Workshop on Scalable Natural Language Understanding 2006

(ScaNaLU 2006)

Held at HLT/NAACL 2006

New York, New York, USA
8 June 2006

ISBN: 978-1-61738-489-9

Printed from e-media with permission by:

Curran Associates, Inc.
57 Morehouse Lane
Red Hook, NY 12571
www.proceedings.com

Some format issues inherent in the e-media version may also appear in this print version.

Printed by Curran Associates, Inc. (2010)

Association for Computational Linguistics
209 N. Eighth Street
Stroudsburg, Pennsylvania 18360

Phone: 1-570-476-8006
Fax: 1-570-476-0860

acl@aclweb.org

Introduction

This volume contains the papers presented at the HLT/NAACL 2006 workshop entitled: Scalable Natural Language Understanding. The workshop was held on June 8th, 2006 and is the third in a series that started in Heidelberg, Germany on May 23rd and 24th 2002 and continued on May 6th, 2004 at HLT/NAACL in Boston. The papers were refereed by an international panel of experts in the field. The workshop is the second held under the auspices of the HLT/NAACL to be directed at issues concerning the scalability of natural language understanding and generation systems.

There is a growing need for systems that can understand and generate natural language in applications that require substantial amounts of knowledge as well as reasoning capabilities. Most current implemented systems for natural language understanding (NLU) are decoupled from any reasoning processes, which makes them narrow and brittle. Furthermore, they do not appear to be scalable in the sense that the techniques used in such systems do not appear to generalize to more complex applications. While significant work has been done in developing theoretical underpinnings of systems that use knowledge and reasoning (e.g., development of models of linguistic interpretation using abductive reasoning, intention recognition, formal models of dialogue, formal models of lexical and utterance meaning, and utterance planning), it has often proved difficult to utilize such theories in robust working systems.

Another major barrier has been the vast amount of linguistic and world knowledge needed. However, there is now significant progress in compiling the required knowledge, using manual and increasingly automated techniques for ontology and grammar learning. But even as these resources become available, we still lack some key conceptual and computational frameworks that will form the foundation for effective scalable natural language systems, e.g., in terms of incremental processing, dialogical alignment or pragmatics. The collection of researchers who face the challenges involved in scaling human language technology is growing in conjuction with greater efforts to develop systems that robustly interact with users in intuitive and conversational ways.

We wish to thank the organizers of HLT/NAACL 2006 for their professional support and the members of the Program Committee for reviewing the submissions on a very tight schedule.

James Allen, University of Rochester
Jan Alexandersson, German Research Center for Artificial Intelligence, Saarbücken
Jerome Feldman, International Computer Science Institute and University of Berkeley
Robert Porzel, European Media Laboratory, Heidelberg

Organizers:

James Allen, University of Rochester
Jan Alexandersson, German Research Center for Artificial Intelligence, Saarbrücken
Jerome Feldman, International Computer Science Institute and University of Berkeley
Robert Porzel, European Media Laboratory, Heidelberg

Program Committee:

Tilman Becker, German Research Center for Artificial Intelligence, Saarbrücken
Paul Buitelaar, German Research Center for Artificial Intelligence, Saarbrücken
Aldo Gangemi, Laboratory for Applied Ontology, Rome
Dan Gildea, University of Rochester
Gnther Grz, University of Erlangen
Joachim de Beule, University of Brussels
Dan Flickinger, Oslo, Saarland and Stanford Universities
Berenike Loos, European Media Laboratory, Heidelberg
Rainer Malaka, University of Bremen
Tomasz Marciniak, Language Computer Corporation, Richardson, Texas
Vanessa Micelli, European Media Laboratory, Heidelberg
Stanley Peters, Stanford University
Massimo Poesio, University of Essex
Len Schubert, University of Rochester
Hans Uszkoreit, Saarland University
Hans-Peter Zorn, European Media Laboratory, Heidelberg

Invited Speaker:

Luc Steels, University of Brussels and Sony Computer Science Laboratory, Paris

Table of Contents

Conference Program

Thursday, June 8, 2006

8:45–9:00	Welcome: Robert Porzel
	Session 1: Elision, Deep Parsing, and Tutoring
9:00–9:30	Pragmatic Information Extraction from Subject Ellipsis in Informal English: Shigeko Nariyama
9:30–10:00	Backbone Extraction and Pruning for Speeding Up a Deep Parser for Dialogue Systems: Myroslava O. Dzikovska and Carolyn P. Rosé
10:00–10:30	Understanding Complex Natural Language Explanations in Tutorial Applications: Pamela W. Jordan, Maxim Makatchev and Umarani Pappuswamy
10:30–11:00	Coffee Break
	Session 2: Lexica, Ontologies and Metaphors
11:00–11:30	Increasing the Coverage of a Domain-independent Dialogue Lexicon with VERBNET: Benoit Crabbé, Myroslava O. Dzikovska, William de Beaumont and Mary Swift
11:30–12:00	Scaling Natural Language Understanding via User-driven Ontology Learning: Berenike Loos
12:00–12:30	Catching Metaphors: Matt Gedigian, John Bryant, Srini Narayanan, and Branimir Ciric
12:30–14:00	Lunch Break
	Session 3: Formal and Computational Construction Grammar
14:00–14:30	Scaling Construction Grammar up to Production Systems: the Situated Constructional Interpretation Model: Guillaume Pitel
14:30–15:00	Searching for Grammar Right: Vanessa Micelli
15:00–15:30	Embodied Construction Grammar as Layered Modal Languages: Anders Søgaard
15:30–16:00	Coffee Break
	Session 4: Invited Talk, Demo Session and Closure
16:00–16:45	A (very) Brief Introduction to Fluid Construction Grammar: Luc Steels and Joachim de Beule (Invited Talk)
16:45–17:15	Demo Session
17:15–17:30	Discussion (Next Workshop)

Pragmatic information extraction from subject ellipsis in informal English

Shigeko Nariyama
Asia Institute
University of Melbourne
Melbourne Australia
shigeko@unimelb.edu.au

Abstract

Subject ellipsis is one of the characteristics of informal English. The investigation of subject ellipsis in corpora thus reveals an abundance of pragmatic and extra-linguistic information associated with subject ellipsis that enhances natural language understanding. In essence, the presence of subject ellipsis conveys an 'informal' conversation involving 1) an informal 'Topic' as well as familiar/close 'Participants', 2) specific 'Connotations' that are different from the corresponding full sentences: interruptive (ending discourse coherence), polite, intimate, friendly, and less determinate implicatures. This paper also construes linguistic environments that trigger the use of subject ellipsis and resolve subject ellipsis.

1 Introduction

The interpretation of pragmatic information, such as intention, implicature[1], underspecified reference, as well as extra-linguistic information, is a prohibitively difficult task in natural language understanding (NLU) at present. This paper demonstrates that this kind of information can be extracted from a small linguistic phenomenon; that is, subject ellipsis observed in informal English.

Ellipsis has a part in the study of anaphora, as it is often referred to as 'zero anaphora'. Anaphora resolution in English (pronominal resolution in particular, and to lesser extent bridging anaphora) has been a challenging topic for some decades both in NLU and linguistics. In contrast, the study of ellipsis in English centers around VP ellipsis and little discussion has been made on subject of nominal ellipsis (naturally because of its infrequent occurrence in formal written texts), and much less still on pragmatic effects generated from subject ellipsis. The study in NLU has approached the topics (VP ellipsis and pronominal anaphors) with the interest of resolving its referent and coreferencing, while linguistics has more concerned with the organization of discourse coherence.

The goal of this paper is to amalgamate both approaches and interests, and more importantly, to draw implicatures that are generated by subject ellipsis, by delineating various types of pragmatic information associated with subject ellipsis. First, it refutes some of the commonly held misconceptions regarding subject ellipsis (Section 2). Section 3 examines the linguistic environments (types of texts, elided subjects and predicates) that trigger subject ellipsis. It also accounts for resolving the referent of subject ellipsis, as this can cause a problem in English for not having extensive subject-verb agreement. Section 4 construes the type of implicatures that subject ellipsis gives rise to. Section 5 suggests a preliminary procedure.

2 Misconceptions about subject ellipsis

Ellipsis, and anaphora more generally, are said to play a major part in the organisation of conversation and narrative for reasons of economy, dis-

[1] An implicature can be defined as anything that is inferred from an utterance but that is not a condition for the truth of the utterance (Levinson 1983:127).

Proceedings of the 3rd Workshop on Scalable Natural Language Understanding, pages 1–8,
New York City, June 2006. ©2006 Association for Computational Linguistics

course coherence, and style (e.g. Halliday and Hassan, 1976). However, subject ellipsis seems to operate rather differently from anaphor and general ellipsis. The findings of this paper dispute or complement 'economy' and 'discourse coherence' as reasons for its use, in particular, the following commonly believed characteristics on subject ellipsis. They are that subject ellipsis is used for:

1) Economy, for speaking fast
2) Coherence
3) Conversation (i.e. spoken dialogue)
4) Spontaneous (unplanned) speech
5) First person pronoun elided in a declarative and second person in an interrogative

1) Regarding economy, subject ellipsis happens for more than simple reasons of economy. In fact, it is suspected that the speakers of English consciously resort to subject ellipsis when they wish to economize their utterance. If the view of economy is maintained, all subject ellipses would be spoken fast and be observed in every hasty utterance, which is not the case in the corpora. Some subjectless sentences, such as '(It's) been a long time' is often spoken slowly with underling emotions. Rather, subject ellipsis seems to be employed more for conveying different implicatures (see §4) that underlie them, that are different from the corresponding full sentences with overt subject.

2) Regarding discourse coherence, one of the implicatures given rise to by the use of subject ellipsis is 'interruptive' and hence it connotes the speaker's intention to end the current topic or conversation itself (see §4.1), by which in effect discourse coherence is discontinued.

3) The perception that subject ellipsis is found in conversation is inaccurate, as it is also found in many informal written texts, such as diaries, postcards, emails, logs and blogs on the internet.

4) Subject ellipsis is believed to be a result of informal spontaneous utterances without planning and editing, but in fact it is not limited to this type. For example, the automated teller machine of a bank in New Zealand gives out this message at the end of inputting instructions, 'OK. Got that.' This is by no means an unplanned message; in fact it is a prudently planned message for a particular implicature, i.e. to make the response sound friendly.

5) The last misconception, which relates to ellipsis resolution, is that subject ellipsis in English operates on the principle that first person pronoun is elided in a declarative and second person in an interrogative with a rising interrogative intonation, as in "(I) got in late." versus "(You) got in late?" This certainly plays a part in the mechanism of subject ellipsis, and is probably true across languages. However, the corpus analyses found that while first person subject ellipsis is prominent, second person subject ellipsis is rare (see §3.2)

3 Linguistic conditions for subject ellipsis

A missing subject in English[2] is syntactically prominent and hence is relatively easy to mechanically detect. However, for speech data it poses an issue. Some subject ellipses can be marginal between ellipsis and phonetic erosion (e.g. inaudible subject word being spoken sotto voce and quickly), and an appropriate heuristically oriented threshold based on instrumental analysis (e.g. the use of spectrography) must be set up as a criterion for determining ellipsis, although across-the-board 'acoustic correlates' of the subject ellipsis may remain as an equivocal issue. For simplicity and reasons that the main theme of this paper is not the determination of ellipsis itself, this paper considers the transcriptions of spoken texts. Moreover, notwithstanding that the role of prosodic features plays a significant part in determining implicatures, given the scope of this paper, it is basically put aside for future study. Nonetheless, the findings are still meaningful for analyzing informal utterances in the internet domains, such as emails, logs and blogs, the type of text that is increasing exponentially in quantity and importance in NLU particularly for being able to process mechanically.

It is conceded that the description of subject ellipsis in this paper is drawn from small corpora in NLU standards, although covering various types of texts and studies in the literature, so that the findings from this analysis are intended to provide a starting point in the study of the pragmatic information that subject ellipsis prevails.

[2] Subject ellipsis refers to those unexpressed subjects occurring in the sentence initial position, hence excluding subject ellipsis in coordinate structures and non-finite clauses (adverbial clauses, gerundive clauses, and prepositional clauses). This is drawn from the claim that non-syntactically motivated subject ellipsis only occurs in the sentence initial position (McShane 2005, Nariyama 2004, Swales 2002, Cote 1996), except that Haegeman and Ihsane (1999) claim that a diary may exhibit some use of subject ellipsis in embedded clauses.

3.1 Type of texts

Undoubtedly subject ellipsis is a feature of informal register. We would not expect to hear subjectless sentences, for example, at court hearings. Indeed, Swales (2002) examined a corpus of academic speech (MICASE), consisting of 36 speech-events, covering such texts as colloquia, dissertation defenses and lab meetings. He reports that subject ellipsis is rare in formal speech; the highest ratio was found for DEPENDS at 14%, followed by LOOKS at 8.1%.

Swales also notes the dialectal aspect that subject ellipsis is a more prominent feature for British English (also by Cote 1996); the rate of subject ellipsis before DEPENDS is 60% in British English conversation and 30% in American English. Comparing these with 14% in MICASE, subject ellipsis is indeed a character of informal speech.

Further evidence is found in Taylor (2002) in analysing Australian English Corpus (Monash University 1996~1998) that *Gotta* often occurred without an overt subject, all with first person subjects. The contracted forms of lexicon, such *gonna, gotta* and *hafta* (so called 'the quasi-modals'), are undoubtedly representative of casual speech.[3]

However, what may not be so obvious is that an informal register does not license the use of subject ellipsis at all times. The corpus analysis on TV drama scripts (§3.2) found that subject ellipsis had a propensity to emerge at particular scenes and topics where the atmosphere of the scenes is both casual and friendly, while it did not occur with the same speech participants at other scenes and topics. This is plausible from the fact that when asking a favour or showing gratitude, more formal language (i.e. without ellipsis) tends to be used even to close participants. Or colleagues may frequently say "Dunno" and "Doesn't matter" to each other. However, in a situation where one lost his job, he is unlikely to use subjectless sentences in response to a question "What happened?"

3.2 Type of elided referents

Table 1 shows the results of the referent distribution of subject ellipsis from analyzing three corpora: 1) three transcripts of family conversation (FaCon) drawn from Australian English Corpus (Monash University 1996~1998) collecting family interviews about their past holidays (Nariyama 2004); 2) three 30-minute-TV Australian drama transcripts (TV) (Nariyama 2004); 3) Switchboard corpus consisting of telephone conversation on a variety of specified every day topics (Cote 1996).

Referent	FaCon	TV dramas	Switchboard
I	10 (20.4%)	25 (47.2%)	47 (26.0%)
we	2 (4.1%)	0	3 (1.7%)
you	4 (8.2%)	3 (5.6%)	13 (7.2%)
he/she	2 (4.1%)	6 (11.3%)	47 (25.9%)
it	30 (61.2%)	17 (32.1%)	67 (37.0%)
they	1 (2.0%)	2 (3.8%)	4 (2.2%)
Total	49 (100%)	53 (100%)	181 (100%)

Table 1: Type of elided referents and their frequency of occurrence by type of texts

The distributions of 'I' and 'it' are different among the texts; more 'it' and less 'I' in the two corpora than in TV. This is attributed to the fact that the data were drawn from conversations with particular topics rather than a free conversation. Hence many utterances relate to the past mentions of descriptions where the anaphoric use of 'it/he/she' is more relevant (see Table 2 §3.4.1 for the ratio). Nonetheless, what is common among the three is that 1) first person pronoun ellipsis is frequent, 2) second person ellipsis is rare, although the corpora are a collection of dialogues (§3.3).

3.3 Informativeness

Semantic informativeness of a sentence plays a major part in enabling subject ellipsis. It is manifested in two ways: type of verbs & adjectives and the amount of information expressed in a sentence.

3.3.1 Type of verbs and adjectives

Subject ellipsis has a strong association with, and hence is triggered by, particular verbs and adjectives (with or without auxiliary). Swales (2002) found the following verbs to be of such types in MICASE (academic speech corpus): DEPENDS, SEEMS, SOUNDS, LOOKS, TURNS OUT, WANNA, HEARD, SEEN, and GOT.

This does not, however, explain the frequency of first person subject ellipsis and rareness of second person subject ellipsis seen in Table 1. Nariyama

[3] The use of subject ellipsis in non-informal texts is also found (Cote 1996). Recipe and instruction texts constantly elide subject (as well as object). This usage is domain specific and the referent is fixed as a second person subject.

(2004) claims that it is fundamentally an epistemic reasoning (having sufficient knowledge about a statement) that has substantial controls on the appllication of subject ellipsis. The most of the verbs above that come with subject ellipsis require epistemic knowledge and hence first person subject ellipsis. Even when the subject is 'it', the agent (psychological subject) is still first person.

Because of epistemic reasoning, semantically rich and private verbal lexicon can only be used for first person subject, as in the (a) examples, and this makes second person subjectless sentences unacceptable even in an interrogative, as in the (b)s.

(1a) (I'd) love a coffee.
(1b) * (Would you) love a coffee?

(2a) (I'm) feeling fantastic.
(2b) (*) (Are you) feeling fantastic?

(3a) (I) wouldn't mind a coffee.
(3b) (*)(You) wouldn't mind a coffee?

'Love' conveys high degree of preference as well as a request, which is privy and subjective to the speaker. Thus, the speaker can state his own feeling, as well as make a request, but cannot do so for others;[4] hence (1b) is unacceptable; analogously for (2b) and (3b), or 'hate', 'thought', and 'hope'. This unacceptability of sentences with second person subject often remains even with overt subjects.

3.3.2 Amount of information

Analogous to the richness and privy of lexicon, informativeness in terms of amount of information (number of phrases) governs the acceptability of subject ellipsis. It is less restricted for sentences with first person subject as in the (a) examples than non-first person subject as in the (b)s.

(4a) (I) had a good time.
(4b) (Did you) have a good time?
(5a) (I) had a wonderful time.
(5b) (?) (Did you) have a wonderful time?

(6a) (I) had a good time visiting my family in Sydney last week.

(6b) (*) (Did you) have a good time visiting your family in Sydney last week?

[4] Japanese is well documented for having rigid constraints on subjective statements (Nariyama 2003, Aoki 1986, inter alia).

3.4 Referent resolution

The recoverability of referent is the imperative condition on the employment of ellipsis, but English has limited subject-verb agreement. So, how is the referent of elided subject retrieved?

3.4.1 Locational constraint

The results in Table 1 are further examined by the type of subject ellipsis, and are summarized as follows (mostly drawn on the TV corpus):

1) Anaphoric (23/53)
2) Deictic (21/53)
3) Idiomatic (conventionalised usage) (8/53)
4) Expletive 'it' (1/17, c.f. FaCon:2/30)

The corpus analysis concludes that 2) Deictic, 3) Idiomatic (§3.4.2) and 4) Expletive subject ellipses can occur freely, but 1) Anaphoric has a locational restriction to occur immediately after the sentence with the referent, for example:

A: Where's dad?
B: [TV33] (He's) birthday shopping, I bet.
[TV34] (He's) so bad at pretending.

Where the referent is not found in the immediately proceeding sentence, quasi-right dislocation was used to express the subject at the end of the sentence, presumably to ensure that no ambiguity of reference would occur, for instance:

Quasi-right dislocation
A: He's going to do a Thorpey after today.
B: Why? What happened?
A: [TV24] Won the year 7 freestyle, he did.

Although the use of 'it' was frequent in Table 1, the expletive use was rare (See Lappin and Leass (1994) for identifying the expletive use of 'it'.) As mentioned, this is attributed to the type of corpora having specific topics of conversation.

Function of ellipsis	Number (FaCon)	Number (TV)
expletive	2	1
deictic	0	1
anaphoric	28	15
Total	30/49 (61.2%)	17/53 (32.1%)

Table 2: Frequency of the function of 'it'

3.4.2 Complementary distribution

The constraints on informativeness described in §3.3 often produce complementary distribution with regard to the type referent for subject ellipsis, and hence they in turn signal the referent of ellipsis. For example, 'love' is associated with first person subject (7a) and 'like' with second (8a):

(7a) (I'd) **love a coffee**.
(7b) *(I'd) like a coffee.

(8a) (Would you) **like a coffee?**
(8b) *(Would you) love a coffee?

Likewise, idiomatic subjectless expressions are essentially set phrases whose meanings are self-contained in their own right, so that elements in the expressions tend to be fixed in terms of person, the declarative/interrogative, polarity, and verbs. Hence, these constraints resolves the referent of subject ellipsis. For example, 'gonna be long' is strongly associated with second person subject and therefore occurs in interrogatives as in (9a). It sounds odd to be used for first person subject even in a declarative (9b) or with the full sentence (9c). Instead (10a) is likely to be used for the proposition, which in turn is awkward for a second person subject (10b). Thus, it creates complementary distribution.

(9a) (Are you) **gonna be long?**
(9b) *(I'm) gonna to be long.
(9c) ? I'm gonna to be long.

(10a) (I'm) **gonna be a while.**
(10b) (*) (Are you) gonna be a while?

Analogously, 'won't be a minute' is strongly associated with first person in declarative (11a), so that the same with second person (11b) is unacceptable unless it is quoting or parodying the earlier statement. The same goes for 'just be a minute' in (12a) and (12b).

(11a) (I) won't be a minute.
(11b) * (You) won't be a minute?

(12a) (I'll) just be a minute.
(12b) * (You will) just be a minute?

Polarity is also often fixed for a particular expression. For example, (13a) is set for first person subject and negative, so that any variation to it gives rise to an unacceptable sentence; e.g. second person negative interrogative (13b) (unless quoting or parodying what the person has just said), first person non-negative declarative (13c), and second person non-negative interrogative (13d) are all unacceptable. Interestingly, (13d) will be acceptable if it is expressed slightly differently with an overt subject, as in "Do you mind having a coffee (because I haven't got anything else at the moment)?"

(13a) (I) wouldn't mind a coffee.
(13b) * (You) wouldn't mind a coffee?
(13c) * (I) mind a coffee.
(13d) * (You) mind a coffee?

Thus, the constraints on person, declarative/interrogative form, polarity, and verbal semantics in turn allow little ambiguity in recovering the referent of subject ellipsis.

3.4.3 Discerning subject ellipsis from imperatives

Subject ellipsis in the initial position is structurally identical with the imperative construction in English. However, potential ambiguities in the interpretation are resolved by a number of factors. First, the semantic content of privy verbs cannot be forced upon someone else, and hence does not make sense for such subjectless sentences to be interpreted as imperatives, for instance:

(14) * Like a coffee!
c.f. (14a) Have a coffee!
(15) * Feel alright!

The second is the tense complementarity. Some verbs tend to occur in a past tense, e.g. 'got', while imperatives do not allow past tense:

(16a) * Got a house!
(16b) Get a house!

The third is that the presence and type of the object can make the distinction; e.g, "Tell you" will be interpreted as a subjectless sentence "(I'll) tell you", while "Tell me" will be interpreted as an imperative "(You) tell me". Analogously, "See you later" is interpreted as a subjectless sentence "(I'll) see you later", while "See me later" as an imperative/request sentence "(You) see me later."

4 Five basic implicatures

Undoubtedly intonation and context play a large part in the inferred meanings. Nonetheless, the iconicity in the implicatures is observed in the following sets of examples. (a)s with subject ellipsis convey specific meanings without being linguistically expressed in a strict sense, while (b)s convey unmarked linguistic meaning.

(17a) (I've) gotta go.
(17b) I've got to go.

(18a) (I) dunno.
(18b) I don't know.

(19a) (I've) got it.
(19b) I've got it.

(20a) (It) doesn't matter.
(20b) It doesn't matter.

(21a) (I) should've known better.
(21b) I should have known better.

(22a) (It's) been a long time.
(22b) It's been a long time.

(17a): a more evasive and dismissive motive,
(17b): tends to imply a more honest/genuine statement that the speaker actually has to get to a particular place by certain time.
(18a): an indeterminate state of mind such as 'I'm not sure', 'I haven't thought about it', or a dismissive motive, such as 'I don't want to think about it.', or even to the extent, 'I don't care'.
(18b): more genuine: 'I thought about it, but I have no idea.'
(19a): more emphatic and the speaker may have anticipated what the interlocutor has just said and therefore (19a) is a little hasty-sounding.
(20a): more likely about trivial matters
(20b): for more important, serious matters, and for giving consolation.
(21a): less directed/emphatic and therefore less punitive and apologetic that the mistake is understandable, silly, or trivial.
(22a): has a restricted usage directed at someone intimate to the speaker.

Five basic implicatures can be drawn from the above and the earlier examples: 1) Interruptive with dismissive/evasive motives (e.g. all of the above except 22a), 2) Polite (e.g. 21a), 3) Intimate (e.g. 22a), 4) Friendly (e.g. 1a, 9a, 19a), and 5) Less determinate implicatures (e.g. 18a, 'Depends', 'Seems').

Subject seems to drop for two basic reasons. First, for 1), 4) and 5) implicatures, the meaning conveyed by subjectless utterances tends to be evasive, less determinate (informative, definite, formal), and spoken fast. It is a logical tendency for semantically insignificant elements to be unstressed, and unstressed pronouns drop, which is economical in conversation. The other is that the subject is intentionally underspecified either for disguising the identity for 2), or for the effect that the absence of the subject makes the identity conspicuous for 3).

4.1 Interruptive implicatures with dismissive/evasive motives

Speech act participants generally have the intention to converse with one another and sustain their conversation, as described in Grice's hallmark discovery of the Cooperative principle (1975). While full sentences to some degree elicit responses from the addressees and therefore aid conversation flow, the corresponding subjectless sentences tend to convey to the addressee implicatures of fulfilling social obligation, keeping a low conversational profile, and minimising invitation of response to the subjectless utterance. For example, "(I've) gotta go" tend to imply that the speaker is fulfilling his social obligation by acknowledging the presence of the addressee in making an utterance, but at the same time indicating that he is not inviting any meaningful response. Indeed, this example was used in the TV drama instead of saying "Good-bye".

If this view is maintained, subject ellipsis can have the effect of changing a topic or ending a conversation itself, in which case it has the opposite effect to what has been claimed on anaphora and ellipsis; anaphora is one means of establishing coherence (e.g. Fox 1996, Halliday and Hasan 1976). This claim is plausible that the use of ellipsis does create cognitive states of coherence on the grounds that the addressee has to look elsewhere for the interpretation of the missing subject; and in doing so links the current sentence to another sentence. It is certainly true for anaphoric use of subjectless sentences, but for the above usages it is questionable.

4.2 Polite implicatures

Some subjects seem deliberately unspecified in order to conceal the subject identity or make it ambiguous for politeness; for example. (Note that in (23) concord is also taken out.)

(23) (I/you/we/he/they/.. 've/s) got to have a coffee.
(24) (I/you/we/he/they/...) should've known better.
(25) (I/you/he/they/...) haven't/hasn't got a chance.
(26) (I/you/we/he/they/...) should send a postcard.

The subject of (23) can be interpreted as anyone in the presence of a group of people, but the intended referent may in fact be 'I' because 'I'm tired', 'you' because 'you look sleepy', or 'we' because 'we all worked so hard'. This under-specified subject avoids a direct speech act and one's responsibility/accusation/self-centeredness (e.g. 'I got to have a coffee'), and softens the implicatures by creating an indirect request/suggestion. Even when the intended referent is clear, it is left up to the addressees whether or not to interpret the elided subject as being directed to himself. This indirectness is seen as one type of politeness strategy (Brown and Levinson 1987, Leech 1983).

(27b) is an interesting example from the TV corpus for having the first person subject ellipsis instead of second in an interrogative '(Would you) like another?', which may contribute to the rareness of second person subject. The same speaker uttered (27a) and (27b) with no pause in between.

(27a) (It) looks cold. [The speaker is looking at the addressee's cup of tea.]
(27b) (Shall I) **make another** (cuppa)?

While the semantic content of the sentences is virtually identical, some speakers of English find (27b) more polite than the one with the second person subject, because it offers help as well as asks the desire of the addressee. This view is consistent with the description by Leech (1983) that the more benefit an utterance brings to the hearer, the more polite it is. Interestingly, (27b) cannot be interpreted as '(Would you) make another?' in the context.

4.3 Intimate implicatures

Some subjectless sentences convey intimate implicatures, when spoken slowly with specific prosody.

(28) (It's) been a long time.
(29) (It's) nice to see you.
(30) (It's) lovely to get your email.

4.4 Friendly implicatures

Subjectless sentences with friendly implicatures relate to particular expressions, such as 'Had a good time' and 'Like a coffee?'

Friendly and Intimate implicatures overlap somewhat, but they differ with the view that the subject in the former drops for being friendly and therefore causal, while in the latter the absence of the subject makes the obvious identity of the subject conspicuous, more meaningful, and private.

4.5 Less determinate implicatures

Owing to the semantics of the verbs, subjectless sentences with such verbs as DEPENDS, SEEMS, SOUNDS, LOOKS, TURNS OUT, HEARD, and SEEN tend to convey less determinate, definite, less objective implicatures. Arnold Zwicky makes similar notes (Language log March 19 2005), in that 'Odd that Mary never showed up' is more expressive/subjective, while the corresponding full sentence 'It is odd that Mary never showed up' is more reportive/objective.

4.6 Discriminating the implicatures

All things in pragmatics are extremely convoluted involving seemingly limitless factors that influence the ultimate interpretation, and worse still all interpretations are defeasible. Thus, the following is a rough description of features that discriminate the five implicatures at this stage.

Each implicature relates to particular expressions deriving from their lexical semantics, particularly the polite and intimate implicatures. Some expressions such as 'Got it' can have multiple implicatures. The qualitative studies with prosodic features will reveal the type of expressions associated with each implicature, for example, the fast spoken 'Got it' is to imply interruptive implicature.

Then the derived implicatures can in turn signal, for example, that the polite implicatures are associated with multiple interpretations of the subject identity (in which case ellipsis resolution is less important for this type of ellipsis), or that the intimate implicatures reveal the speaker's loving relationship with the addressee.

5 Resolution procedure

A preliminary rough procedure regarding subject ellipsis in English is briefly suggested here.

1. *Detect* a sentence-initial subject ellipsis.
   1.1 Discard if it is an imperative based on §3.4.3.
2. *Pragmatic information extraction*
   Draw an implicature based on §4.6 with consideration to the dialectal differences (§3.1).
3. *Extra linguistic information extraction*
   Sublectless sentsences imply 'informal' conversation involving an informal 'topic' and familiar/close 'participants'.

6 Conclusion

This paper has made a wide description concerning subject ellipsis in English: the linguistic environments that trigger subject ellipsis, including the subject ellipsis resolution, and the marked implicatures conveyed by subject ellipsis that are different from those given by the corresponding full sentences with overt subject. It seems paradoxical that less words, i.e. more ellipses, convey more internal feelings and intentions.

Subject ellipsis, and elliptical constructions more generally, are an essential feature of everyday conversation and are a common phenomenon cross-linguistically. Gilligan (1987) reported, based on a sample of 100 languages, that only seven of these do not allow subject ellipsis in finite clauses. Since English is not generally known for ellipsis, the study on other languages may reveal more interesting outcomes.

Finally, the work on this topic is in its infancy and great more work ahead of us before the findings can be put to meaningful use in an NLU system. First, a quantitative investigation with prosodic features is a must for assuring the findings of this paper and creating an inventory of subject ellipsis. Further investigation will point to the direction for the most appropriate applications and methods to implement this sort of pragmatic information into a system. The use of findings may be more accurate and feasible for generation than for understanding. Nonetheless, it will be of use to applications that are in search of contextual cues to identifying the type of topic, participants and their relationship, and in rephrasing relatively formal sentences to more informal ones.

References

Haruo Aoki. 1986. Evidentials in Japanese. In Chafe & Nichols (eds). *Evidentiality: the linguistic coding of epistemology*. Norwood: Ablex 223-238

Penelope Brown and Stephen Levinson. 1987. *Politeness: some universals in language usage*. Cambridge: Cambridge University Press.

Cote Sharon. 1996. *Grammatical and Discourse Properties of Null Arguments in English*, Ph.D. Dissertation, University of Pennsylvania.

Barbara Fox. 1996. *Studies in anaphora*. Typological studies in language 33. Amsterdam: John Benjamins.

Gary Gilligan. 1987. *A cross-linguistic approach to the pro-drop parameter*, University of Southern California Dissertation.

Paul H. Grice. 1975. Logic and conversation. In P. Cole & J.L. Morgan eds., *Syntax and semantics 3: Speech Acts*. 43-58, New York: Academic Press.

M.S.K. Halliday and R. Hasan, 1976. *Cohesion in English*. London: Longman.

Shalom Lappin and Herbert Leass. 1994. An algorithm for pronominal anaphora resolution. *Computational Linguistics,* 20(4): 535-561.

Geoffrey Leech. 1983. *Principle of pragmatics*. London: Longman.

Stephen Levinson. 1983. *Pragmatics*. Cambridge: Cambridge University Press.

Liliane Haegeman and Tabea Ihsane. 1999. Subject ellipsis in embedded clauses in English, *English Language and Linguistics*, 3(1): 117-145.

Marjorie McShane. 2005. *A theory of ellipsis*. Oxford University Press.

Shigeko Nariyama. 2003. *Ellipsis and Reference-tracking in Japanese*. Studies in Language Companion Series 66, Amsterdam: John Benjamins

Shigeko Nariyama. 2004. Subject ellipsis in English, *Journal of Pragmatics*, 36(2): 237-264.

John Swales. 2002. "Any last minute thoughts on this particular search?" The occurrence of sentence-initial ellipsis in research speech. In Proc. of the 4th North American Symposium on corpus linguistics and language teaching.

Jo Taylor. 2002. The quasi-modals *gonna, gotta* and *hafta* in Australian English. paper presented at Australian Linguistic Society Annual Meeting at Macquarie University Sydney.

Backbone Extraction and Pruning for Speeding Up a Deep Parser for Dialogue Systems

Myroslava O. Dzikovska
Human Communication Research Centre
University of Edinburgh
Edinburgh, EH8 9LW, United Kingdom,
mdzikovs@inf.ed.ac.uk

Carolyn P. Rosé
Carnegie Mellon University
Language Technologies Institute,
Pittsburgh, PA 15213,
cprose@cs.cmu.edu

Abstract

In this paper we discuss issues related to speeding up parsing with wide-coverage unification grammars. We demonstrate that state-of-the-art optimisation techniques based on backbone parsing before unification do not provide a general solution, because they depend on specific properties of the grammar formalism that do not hold for all unification based grammars. As an alternative, we describe an optimisation technique that combines ambiguity packing at the constituent structure level with pruning based on local features.

1 Introduction

In this paper we investigate the problem of scaling up a deep unification-based parser developed specifically for the purpose of robust interpretation in dialogue systems by improving its speed and coverage for longer utterances. While typical sentences in dialogue contexts are shorter than in expository text domains, longer utterances are important in discussion oriented domains. For example, in educational applications of dialogue it is important to elicit deep explanation from students and then offer focused feedback based on the details of what students say.

The choice of instructional dialogue as a target application influenced the choice of parser we needed to use for interpretation in a dialogue system. Several deep, wide-coverage parsers are currently available (Copestake and Flickinger, 2000; Rosé, 2000; Baldridge, 2002; Maxwell and Kaplan, 1994), but many of these have not been designed with issues related to interpretation in a dialogue context in mind.

The TRIPS grammar (Dzikovska et al., 2005) is a wide-coverage unification grammar that has been used very successfully in several task-oriented dialogue systems. It supports interpretation of fragments and lexical semantic features (see Section 2 for a more detailed discussion), and provides additional robustness through "robust" rules that cover common grammar mistakes found in dialogue such as missing articles or incorrect agreement. These enhancements help parsing dialogue (both spoken and typed), but they significantly increase grammar ambiguity, a common concern in building grammars for robust parsing (Schneider and McCoy, 1998). It is specifically these robustness-efficiency trade-offs that we address in this paper.

Much work has been done related to enhancing the efficiency of deep interpretation systems (Copestake and Flickinger, 2000; Swift et al., 2004; Maxwell and Kaplan, 1994), which forms the foundation that we build on in this work. For example, techniques for speeding up unification in HPSG lead to dramatic improvements in efficiency (Kiefer et al., 1999). Likewise ambiguity packing and CFG backbone parsing (Maxwell and Kaplan, 1994; van Noord, 1997) are known to increase parsing efficiency. However, as we show in this paper, these techniques depend on specific grammar properties that do not hold for all grammars. This claim is consistent with observations of Carroll (1994) that parsing software optimisation techniques tend to be limited in their applicability to the individual grammars they were developed for. While we used TRIPS as our example unification-based grammar, this investigation is important not only for this project, but in the general context of speeding up a wide-coverage unification grammar which incorporates fragment

Proceedings of the 3rd Workshop on Scalable Natural Language Understanding, pages 9–16,
New York City, June 2006.

rules and lexical semantics, which may not be immediately provided by other available systems.

In the remainder of the paper, we begin with a brief description of the TRIPS parser and grammar, and motivate the choice of LCFLEX parsing algorithm to provide a fast parsing foundation. We then discuss the backbone extraction and pruning techniques that we used, and evaluate them in comparison with the original parsing algorithm. We conclude with discussion of some implications for implementing grammars that build deep syntactic and semantic representations.

2 Motivation

The work reported in this paper was done as part of the process of developing a dialogue system that incorporates deep natural language understanding. We needed a grammar that provides lexical semantic interpretation, supports parsing fragmentary utterance in dialogue, and could be used to start development without large quantities of corpus data. TRIPS fulfilled our requirements better than similar alternatives, such as LINGO ERG (Copestake and Flickinger, 2000) or XLE (Maxwell and Kaplan, 1994).

TRIPS produces logical forms which include semantic classes and roles in a domain-independent frame-based formalism derived from FrameNet and VerbNet (Dzikovska et al., 2004; Kipper et al., 2000). Lexical semantic features are known to be helpful in both deep (Tetreault, 2005) and shallow interpretation tasks (Narayanan and Harabagiu, 2004). Apart from TRIPS, these have not been integrated into existing deep grammars. While both LINGO-ERG and XLE include semantic features related to scoping, in our applications the availability of semantic classes and semantic role assignments was more important to interpretation, and these features are not currently available from those parsers. Finally, TRIPS provides a domain-independent parse selection model, as well as rules for interpreting discourse fragments (as was also done in HPSG (Schlangen and Lascarides, 2003), a feature actively used in interpretation.

While TRIPS provides the capabilities we need, its parse times for long sentences (above 15 words long) are intolerably long. We considered two possible techniques for speeding up parsing: speeding up unification using the techniques similar to the LINGO system (Copestake and Flickinger, 2000), or using backbone extraction (Maxwell and Kaplan, 1994; Rosé and Lavie, 2001; Briscoe and Carroll, 1994). TRIPS already uses a fast unification algorithm similar to quasi-destructive unification, avoiding copying during unification.[1] However, the TRIPS grammar retains the notion of phrase structure, and thus it was more natural to chose to use backbone extraction with ambiguity packing to speed up the parsing.

As a foundation for our optimisation work, we started with the freely available LCFLEX parser (Rosé and Lavie, 2001). LCFLEX is an all-paths parser that uses left-corner prediction and ambiguity packing to make all-paths parsing tractable, and which was shown to be efficient for long sentences with somewhat less complex unification augmented context-free grammars. We show that all-paths parsing with LCFLEX is not tractable for the ambiguity level in the TRIPS grammar, but that by introducing a pruning method that uses ambiguity packing to guide pruning decisions, we can achieve significant improvements in both speed and coverage compared to the original TRIPS parser.

3 The TRIPS and LCFLEX algorithms

3.1 The TRIPS parser

The TRIPS parser we use as a baseline is a bottom-up chart parser with lexical entries and rules represented as attribute-value structures. To achieve parsing efficiency, TRIPS uses a best-first beam search algorithm based on the scores from a parse selection model (Dzikovska et al., 2005; Elsner et al., 2005). The constituents on the parser's agenda are grouped into buckets based on their scores. At each step, the bucket with the highest scoring constituents is selected to build/extend chart edges. The parsing stops once N requested analyses are found. This guarantees that the parser returns the N-best list of analyses according to the parse selection model used, unless the parser reaches the chart size limit.

[1] Other enhancements used by LINGO depend on disallowing disjunctive features, and relying instead on the type system. The TRIPS grammar is untyped and uses disjunctive features, and converting it to a typed system would require as yet undetermined amount of additional work.

In addition to best-first parsing, the TRIPS parser uses a chart size limit, to prevent the parser from running too long on unparseable utterances, similar to (Frank et al., 2003). TRIPS is much slower processing utterances not covered in the grammar, because it continues its search until it reaches the chart limit. Thus, a lower chart limit improves parsing efficiency. However, we show in our evaluation that the chart limit necessary to obtain good performance in most cases is too low to find parses for utterances with 15 or more words, even if they are covered by the grammar.

The integration of lexical semantics in the TRIPS lexicon has a major impact on parsing in TRIPS. Each word in the TRIPS lexicon is associated with a semantic type from a domain-independent ontology. This enables word sense disambiguation and semantic role labelling for the logical form produced by the grammar. Multiple word senses result in additional ambiguity on top of syntactic ambiguity, but it is controlled in part with the use of weak selectional restrictions, similar to the restrictions employed by the VerbNet lexicon (Kipper et al., 2000). Checking semantic restrictions is an integral part of TRIPS parsing, and removing them significantly decreases speed and increases ambiguity of the TRIPS parser (Dzikovska, 2004). We show that it also has an impact on parsing with a CFG backbone in Section 4.1.

3.2 LCFLEX

The LCFLEX parser (Rosé and Lavie, 2001) is an all-paths robust left corner chart parser designed to incorporate various robustness techniques such as word skipping, flexible unification, and constituent insertion. Its left corner chart parsing algorithm is similar to that described by Briscoe and Carroll (1994). The system supports grammatical specification in a unification framework that consists of context-free grammar rules augmented with feature bundles associated with the non-terminals of the rules. LCFLEX can be used in two parsing modes: either context-free parsing can be done first, followed by applying the unification rules, or unification can be done interleaved with context-free parsing. The context free backbone allows for efficient left corner predictions using a pre-compiled left corner prediction table, such as that described in (van Noord, 1997). To enhance its efficiency, it incorporates a provably optimal ambiguity packing algorithm (Lavie and Rosé, 2004).

These efficiency techniques make feasible all-path parsing with the LCFLEX CARMEL grammar (Rosé, 2000). However, CARMEL was engineered with fast all-paths parsing in mind, resulting in certain compromises in terms of coverage. For example, it has only very limited coverage for noun-noun compounding, or headless noun phrases, which are a major source of ambiguity with the TRIPS grammar.

4 Combining LCFLEX and TRIPS

4.1 Adding CFG Backbone

A simplified TRIPS grammar rule for verb phrases and a sample verb entry are shown in Figure 1. The features for building semantic representations are omitted for brevity. Each constituent has an assigned category that corresponds to its phrasal type, and a set of (complex-valued) features.

The backbone extraction algorithm is reasonably straightforward, with CFG non-terminals corresponding directly to TRIPS constituent categories. To each CFG rule we attach a corresponding TRIPS unification rule. After parsing is complete, the parses found are scored and ordered with the parse selection model, and therefore parsing accuracy in all-paths mode is the same or better than TRIPS accuracy for the same model.

For constituents with subcategorized arguments (verbs, nouns, adverbial prepositions), our backbone generation algorithm takes the subcategorization frame into account. For example, the TRIPS VP rule will split into 27 CFG rules corresponding to different subcategorization frames: VP → V_intr, VP → V_NP NP, VP → V_NP_CP NP CP, *etc.* For each lexical entry, its appropriate CFG category is determined based on the subcategorization frame from TRIPS lexical representation. This improves parsing efficiency using the prediction algorithms in TFLEX operating on the CFG backbone. The version of the TRIPS grammar used in testing contained 379 grammar rules with 21 parts of speech (terminal symbols) and 31 constituent types (non-terminal symbols), which were expanded into 1121 CFG rules with 85 terminals and 36 non-terminals during backbone extraction.

We found, however, that the previously used tech-

```
(a) ((VP (SUBJ ?!subj) (CLASS ?lf))
    -vp1-role .99
    (V (LF ?lf) (SUBJ ?!subj) (DOBJ ?dobj)
              (IOBJ ?iobj) (COMP3 ?comp3))
    ?iobj ?dobj ?comp3)
(b) ((V (agr 3s) (LF LF::Filling)
    (SUBJ (NP (agr 3s)))
    (DOBJ (NP (case obj))) (IOBJ -) (COMP3 -)))
```

Figure 1: (a) A simplified VP rule from the TRIPS grammar; (b) a simplified verb entry for a transitive verb. Question marks denote variables.

nique of context-free parsing first followed by full re-unification was not suitable for parsing with the TRIPS grammar. The CFG structure extracted from the TRIPS grammar contains 43 loops resulting from lexical coercion rules or elliptical constructions. A small number of loops from lexical coercion were both obvious and easy to avoid, because they are in the form *N*→ *N*. However, there were longer loops, for example, *NP* → *SPEC* for sentences like "John's car" and *SPEC* → *NP* for headless noun phrases in sentences like "I want three". LCFLEX uses a re-unification algorithm that associates a set of unification rules with each CFG production, which are reapplied at a later stage. To be able to apply a unification rule corresponding to *N*→ *N* production, it has to be explicitly present in the chart, leading to an infinite number of *N* constituents produced. Applying the extra CFG rules expanding the loops during re-unification would complicate the algorithm significantly. Instead, we implemented loop detection during CFG parsing.

The feature structures prevent loops in unification, and we considered including certain grammatical features into backbone extraction as done in (Briscoe and Carroll, 1994). However, in the TRIPS grammar the feature values responsible for breaking loops belonged to multi-valued features (6 valued in the worst case), with values which may depend on other multiple-valued features in daughter constituents. Thus adding the extra features resulted in major backbone size increases because of category splitting. This can be remedied with additional pre-compilation (Kiefer and Krieger, 2004), however, this requires that all lexical entries be known in advance. One nice feature of the TRIPS lexicon is that it includes a mechanism for dynamically adding lexical entries for unknown words from wide-coverage lexicons such as VerbNet (Kipper et al., 2000), which would be impractical to use in pre-compilation.

Therefore, to use CFG parsing before unification in our system, we implemented a loop detector that checked the CFG structure to disallow loops. However, the next problem that we encountered is massive ambiguity in the CFG structure. Even a very short phrase such as "a train" had over 700 possible CFG analyses, and took 910 msec to parse compared to 10 msec with interleaved unification. CFG ambiguity is so high because noun phrase fragments are allowed as top-level categories, and lexical ambiguity is compounded with semantic ambiguity and robust rules normally disallowed by features during unification. Thus, in our combined algorithm we had to use unification interleaved with parsing to filter out the CFG constituents.

4.2 Ambiguity Packing

For building semantic representations in parallel with parsing, ambiguity packing presents a set of known problems (Oepen and Carroll, 2000). One possible solution is to exclude semantic features during an initial unification stage, use ambiguity packing, and re-unify with semantic features in a post-processing stage. In our case, we found this strategy difficult to implement, since selectional restrictions are used to limit the ambiguity created by multiple word senses during syntactic parsing. Therefore, we chose to do ambiguity packing on the CFG structure only, keeping the multiple feature structures associated with each packed CFG constituent.

To begin to evaluate the contribution of ambiguity packing on efficiency, we ran a test on the first 39 utterances in a hold out set not used in the formal evaluation below. Sentences ranged from 1 to 17 words in length, 16 of which had 6 or more words. On this set, the average parse time without ambiguity packing was 10 seconds per utterance, and 30 seconds per utterance on utterances with 6 or more words. With ambiguity packing turned on, the average parse time decreased to 5 seconds per utterance, and 13.5 seconds per utterance on the utterances with more than 6 words. While this evaluation showed that ambiguity packing improves parsing efficiency, we determined that further enhancements were necessary.

4.3 Pruning

We added a pruning technique based on the scoring model discussed above and ambiguity packing to enhance system performance. As an illustration, consider an example from a corpus used in our evaluation where the TRIPS grammar generates a large number of analyses, "we have a heart attack victim at marketplace mall". The phrase "a heart attack victim" has at least two interpretations,"a [N1 heart [N1 attack [N1 victim]]]" and "a [N1 [N1 heart [N1 attack]] [N1 victim]]". The prepositional phrase "at marketplace mall" can attach either to the noun phrase or to the verb. Overall, this results in 4 basic interpretations, with additional ambiguity resulting from different possible senses of "have".

The best-first parsing algorithm in TRIPS uses parse selection scores to suppress less likely interpretations. In our example, the TRIPS parser will chose the higher-scoring one of the two interpretations for "a heart attack victim", and use it first. For this NP the features associated with both interpretations are identical with respect to further processing, thus TRIPS will never come back to the other interpretation, effectively pruning it. "At" also has 2 possible interpretations due to word sense ambiguity: LF::TIME-LOC and LF::SPATIAL-LOC. The former has a slightly higher preference, and TRIPS will try it first. But then it will be unable to find an interpretation for "at Marketplace Mall", and backtrack to LF::SPATIAL-LOC to find a correct parse.

Without chart size limits the parser is guaranteed to find a parse eventually through backtracking. However, this algorithm does not work quite as well with chart size limits. If there are many similarly-scored constituents in the chart for different parts of the utterance, the best-first algorithm expands them first, and the the chart size limit tends to interfere before TRIPS can backtrack to an appropriate lower-scoring analysis.

Ambiguity packing offers an opportunity to make pruning more strategic by focusing specifically on competing interpretations for the same utterance span. The simplest pruning idea would be for every ambiguity packed constituent to eliminate the interpretations with low TRIPS scores. However, we need to make sure that we don't prune constituents that are required higher up in the tree to make a parse. Consider our example again.

The constituent for "at" will be ambiguity packed with its two meanings. But if we prune LF::SPATIAL-LOC at that point, the parse for "at Marketplace Mall" will fail later. Formally, the competing interpretations for "at" have *n*on-local features, namely, the subcategorized complement (time versus location) is different for those interpretations, and is checked higher up in the parse. But for "a heart attack victim" the ambiguity-packed interpretations differ only in local features. All features associated with this NP checked higher up come from the head noun "victim" and are identical in all interpretations. Therefore we can eliminate the low scoring interpretations with little risk of discarding those essential for finding a complete parse. Thus, for any constituent where ambiguity-packed non-head daughters differ only in local features, we prune the interpretations coming from them to a specified prune beam width based on their TRIPS scores.

This pruning heuristic based on local features can be generalised to different unification grammars. For example, in HPSG pruning would be safe at all points where a head is combined with ambiguity-packed non-head constituents, due to the locality principle. In the TRIPS grammar, if a trips rule uses subcategorization features, the same locality principle holds. This heuristic has perfect precision though not complete recall, but, as our evaluation shows, it is sufficient to significantly improve performance in comparison with the TRIPS parser.

5 Evaluation

The purpose of our evaluation is to explore the extent to which we can achieve a better balance between parse time and coverage using backbone parsing with pruning compared to the original best-first algorithm. For our comparison we used an excerpt from the Monroe corpus that has been used in previous TRIPS research on parsing speed and accuracy (Swift et al., 2004) consisting of dialogues s2, s4, s16 and s17. Dialogue s2 was a hold out set used for pilot testing and setting parameters. The other three dialogues were set aside for testing. Altogether, the test set contained 1042 utterances, ranging from 1 to

45 words in length (mean 5.38 words/utt, st. dev. 5.7 words/utt). Using our hold-out set, we determined that a beam width of three was an optimal setting. Thus, we compared TFLEX using a beam width of 3 to three different versions of TRIPS that varied only in terms of the maximum chart size, giving us a version that is significantly faster than TFLEX overall, one that has parse times that are statistically indistinguishable from TFLEX, and one that is significantly slower. We show that while lower chart sizes in TRIPS yield speed ups in parse time, they come with a cost in terms of coverage.

5.1 Evaluation Methodology

Because our goal is to explore the parse time versus coverage trade-offs of two different parsing architectures, the two evaluation measures that we report are average parse time per sentence and probability of finding at least one parse, the latter being a measure estimating the effect of parse algorithm on parsing coverage.

Since the scoring model is the same in TRIPS and TFLEX, then as long as TFLEX can find at least one parse (which happened in all but 1 instances on our held-out set), the set returned will include the one produced by TRIPS. We spot-checked the TFLEX utterances in the test set for which TRIPS could not find a parse to verify that the parses produced were reasonable. The parses produced by TFLEX on these sentences were typically acceptable, with errors mainly stemming from attachment disambiguation problems.

5.2 Results

We first compared parsers in terms of probability of producing at least one parse (see Figure 2). Since the distribution of sentence lengths in the test corpus was heavily skewed toward shorter sentences, we grouped sentences into equivalence classes based on a range of sentence lengths with a 5-word increment, with all of the sentences over 20 words aggregated in the same class. Given a large number of short sentences, there was no significant difference overall in likelihood to find a parse. However, on sentences greater than 10 words long, TFLEX is significantly more likely to produce a parse than any of the TRIPS parsers (evaluated using a binary logistic regression, $N = 334$, $G = 16.8$, $DF = 1$, $p < .001$). Furthermore, for sentences greater than 20 words long, no form of TRIPS parser ever returned a complete parse.

Parser	<= 20 words	>= 6 words
TFLEX	6.2 (20.2)	29.1 (96.3)
TRIPS-1500	2.3 (5.4)	6.9 (8.2)
TRIPS-5000	7.7 (30.2)	28.1 (56.4)
TRIPS-10000	22.7 (134.4)	107.6 (407.4)

Table 1: The average parse times for TRIPS and TFLEX on utterances 6 words or more.

Next we compared the parsers in terms of average parse time on the whole data set across equivalence classes of sentences, assigned based on Aggregated Sentence Length (see Figure 2 and Table 1). An ANOVA with Parser and Aggregated Sentence Length as independent variables and Parse Time as the dependent variable showed a significant effect of Parser on Parse Time ($F(3, 4164) = 270.03$, $p < .001$). Using a Bonferroni post-hoc analysis, we determined that TFLEX is significantly faster than TRIPS-10000 ($p < .001$), statistically indistinguishable in terms of parse time from TRIPS-5000, and significantly slower than TRIPS-1500 ($p < .001$). Since none of the TRIPS parsers ever returned a parse for sentences greater than 20 words long, we recomputed this analysis excluding the latter. We still find a significant effect of Parser on Parse Time ($F(3, 4068) = 18.6$, $p < .001$). However, a post-hoc analysis reveals that parse times for TFLEX, TRIPS-1500, and TRIPS-5000 are statistically indistinguishable for this subset, whereas TFLEX is significantly faster than TRIPS-10000 ($p < .001$). See Table 1 for for parse times of all four parsers. Since TFLEX and TRIPS both spent 95% of their computational effort on sentences with 6 or more words, we also include results for this subset of the corpus.

Thus, TFLEX presents a superior balance of coverage and efficiency especially for long sentences (10 words or more) since for these sentences it is significantly more likely to find a parse than any version of TRIPS, even a version where the chart size is expanded to an extent that it becomes significantly slower (i.e., TRIPS-10000). And while TRIPS-1500 is consistently faster than the other parsers, it is not significantly faster than TFLEX on sentences 20

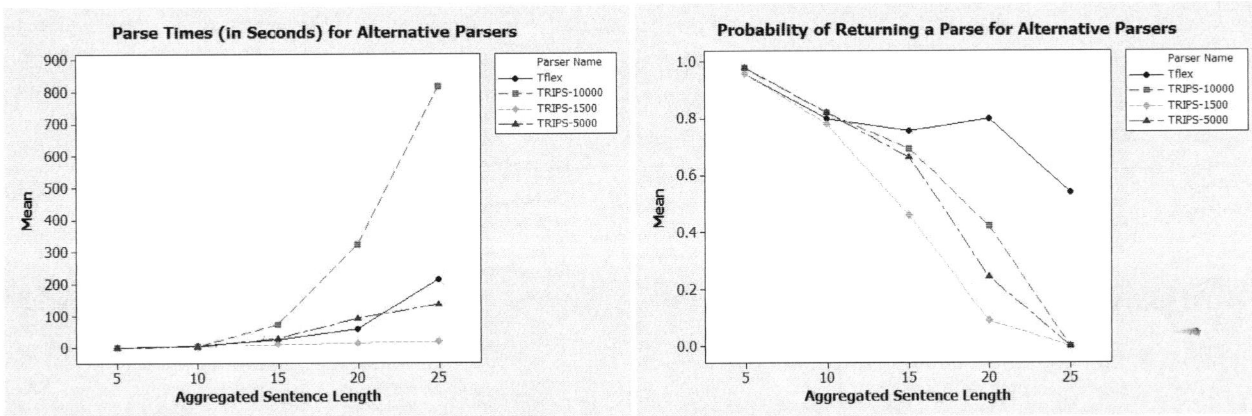

Figure 2: Parse times and probability of getting a parse depending on (aggregated) sentence lengths. 5 denotes sentences with 5 or fewer words, 25 sentences with more than 20 words.

words long or less, which is the subset of sentences for which it is able to find a parse.

5.3 Discussion and Future Work

The most obvious lesson learned in this experience is that the speed up techniques developed for specific grammars and unification formalisms do not transfer easily to other unification grammars. The features that make TRIPS interesting – the inclusion of lexical semantics, and the rules for parsing fragments – also make it less amenable to using existing efficiency techniques.

Grammars with an explicit CFG backbone normally restrict the grammar writer from writing grammar loops, a restriction not imposed by general unification grammars. As we showed, there can be a substantial number of loops in a CFG due to the need to cover various elliptical constructions, which makes CFG parsing not interleaved with unification less attractive in cases where we want to avoid expensive CFG precompilation. Moreover, as we found with the TRIPS grammar, in the context of robust parsing with lexical semantics the ambiguity in a CFG backbone grows large enough to make CFG parsing followed by unification inefficient. We described an alternative technique that uses pruning based on a parse selection model.

Another option for speeding up parsing that we have not discussed in detail is using a typed grammar without disjunction and speeding up unification as done in HPSG grammars (Kiefer et al., 1999). In order to do this, we must first address the issue of integrating the type of lexical semantics that we require with HPSG's type system. Adding lexical semantics while retaining the speed benefits obtained through this type system would require that the semantic type ontology be expressed in the same formalism as the syntactic types. We plan to further explore this option in our future work.

Though longer sentences were relatively rare in our test set, using the system in an educational domain (our ultimate goal) means that the longer sentences are particularly important, because they often correspond to significant instructional events, specifically answers to deep questions such as "why" and "how" questions. Our evaluation has been designed to show system performance with utterances of different length, which would roughly correspond to the performance in interpreting short and long student answers. Since delays in responding can de-motivate the student and decrease the quality of the dialogue, improving handling of long utterances can have an important effect on the system performance. Evaluating this in practice is a possible direction for future work.

6 Conclusions

We described a combination of efficient parsing techniques to improve parsing speed and coverage with the TRIPS deep parsing grammar. We showed that context-free parsing was inefficient on a backbone extracted from an existing unification grammar, and demonstrated how to make all-path parsing more tractable by a new pruning algorithm based on ambiguity packing and local features, generalisable to other unification grammars. We demonstrated that our pruning algorithm provides better efficiency-coverage balance than the best-first parsing with chart limits utilised by the TRIPS parser, and discussed the design implications for other robust parsing grammars.

Acknowledgements

We thank Mary Swift and James Allen for their help with the TRIPS code and useful comments. This material is based on work supported by grants from the Office of Naval Research under numbers N000140510048 and N000140510043.

References

J. Baldridge. 2002. *Lexically Specified Derivational Control in Combinatory Categorial Grammar*. Ph.D. thesis, University of Edinburgh.

T. Briscoe and J. Carroll. 1994. Generalized probabilistic LR parsing of natural language (corpora) with unification-based grammars. *Computational Linguistics*, 19(1):25–59.

J. Carroll. 1994. Relating complexity to practical performance in parsing with wide-coverage unification grammars. In *Proceedings of ACL-2004*.

A. Copestake and D. Flickinger. 2000. An open source grammar development environment and broad-coverage English grammar using HPSG. In *Proceedings of LREC-2000*, Athens, Greece.

M. O. Dzikovska, M. D. Swift, and J. F. Allen. 2004. Building a computational lexicon and ontology with framenet. In *LREC workshop on Building Lexical Resources from Semantically Annotated Corpora*.

M. Dzikovska, M. Swift, J. Allen, and W. de Beaumont. 2005. Generic parsing for multi-domain semantic interpretation. In *Proceedings of the 9th International Workshop on Parsing Technologies (IWPT-05)*.

M. O. Dzikovska. 2004. *A Practical Semantic Representation For Natural Language Parsing*. Ph.D. thesis, University of Rochester.

M. Elsner, M. Swift, J. Allen, and D. Gildea. 2005. Online statistics for a unification-based dialogue parser. In *Proceedings of the 9th International Workshop on Parsing Technologies (IWPT-05)*.

A. Frank, B. Kiefer, B. Crysmann, M. Becker, and U. Schafer. 2003. Integrated shallow and deep parsing: TopP meets HPSG. In *Proceedings of ACL 2003*.

B. Kiefer and H.-U. Krieger. 2004. A context-free approximation of head-driven phrase structure grammar. In H. Bunt, J. Carroll, and G. Satta, editors, *New Developments in Parsing Technology*. Kluwer.

B. Kiefer, H. Krieger, J. Carroll, and R. Malouf. 1999. Bag of useful techniques for efficient and robust parsing. In *Proceedings of ACL 1999*.

K. Kipper, H. T. Dang, and M. Palmer. 2000. Class-based construction of a verb lexicon. In *Proceedings of the 7th Conference on Artificial Intelligence and of the 12th Conference on Innovative Applications of Artificial Intelligence*.

A. Lavie and C. P. Rosé. 2004. Optimal ambiguity packing in context-free parsers with interleaved unification. In H. Bunt, J. Carroll, and G. Satta, editors, *Current Issues in Parsing Technologies*. Kluwer Academic Press.

J. T. Maxwell and R. M. Kaplan. 1994. The interface between phrasal and functional constraints. *Computational Linguistics*, 19(4):571–590.

S. Narayanan and S. Harabagiu. 2004. Question answering based on semantic structures. In *Proceedings of International Conference on Computational Linguistics (COLING 2004)*, Geneva, Switzerland.

S. Oepen and J. Carroll. 2000. Ambiguity packing in constraint-based parsing - practical results. In *Proceedings of NAACL'00*.

C. P. Rosé and A. Lavie. 2001. Balancing robustness and efficiency in unification-augmented context-free parsers for large practical applications. In J. Junqua and G. Van Noord, editors, *Robustness in Language and Speech Technology*. Kluwer Academic Press.

C. Rosé. 2000. A framework for robust semantic interpretation. In *Proceedings 1st Meeting of the North American Chapter of the Association for Computational Linguistics*.

D. Schlangen and A. Lascarides. 2003. The interpretation of non-sentential utterances in dialogue. In *Proceedings of the 4th SIGdial Workshop on Discourse and Dialogue*, Japan, May.

D. Schneider and K. F. McCoy. 1998. Recognizing syntactic errors in the writing of second language learners. In *Proceedings of COLING-ACL'98*.

M. Swift, J. Allen, and D. Gildea. 2004. Skeletons in the parser: Using a shallow parser to improve deep parsing. In *Proceedings of COLING-04*.

J. Tetreault. 2005. *Empirical Evaluations of Pronoun Resolution*. Ph.D. thesis, University of Rochester.

G. van Noord. 1997. An efficient implementation of the head-corner parser. *Computational Linguistics*, 23(3):425–456.

Understanding Complex Natural Language Explanations in Tutorial Applications*

Pamela W. Jordan, Maxim Makatchev and Umarani Pappuswamy
Learning Research and Development Center
University of Pittsburgh
Pittsburgh PA, 15260
{pjordan,maxim,umarani}@pitt.edu

Abstract

We describe the WHY2-ATLAS intelligent tutoring system for qualitative physics that interacts with students via natural language dialogue. We focus on the issue of analyzing and responding to multi-sentential explanations. We explore an approach that combines a statistical classifier, multiple semantic parsers and a formal reasoner for achieving a deeper understanding of these explanations in order to provide appropriate feedback on them.

1 Introduction

Most natural language tutorial applications have focused on coaching either problem solving or procedural knowledge (e.g. Steve (Johnson and Rickel, 1997), Circsim-tutor (Evens and Michael, 2006), Atlas (Rosé et al., 2001), BEETLE (Zinn et al., 2002), SCoT (Peters et al., 2004), *inter alia*). When coaching problem solving, simple short answer analysis techniques are frequently sufficient because the primary goal is to lead a trainee step-by-step through problem solving. There is a narrow range of possible responses and the context of the previous dialogue and questions invite short answers. But when the instructional objectives shift and a tutorial system attempts to explore a student's chain of reasoning behind an answer or decision, deeper analysis techniques can begin to pay off. Having the student construct more on his own is important for learning perhaps in part because it reveals what the student does and does not understand (Chi et al., 2001).

When the student is invited to provide a longer chain of reasoning, the explanations become multi-sentential. Compare the short explanation in Figure 1 to the longer ones in Figures 2 and 3. The explanation in Figure 2 is part of an actual initial student response and Figure 3 shows the explanation from the same student after a follow-up dialogue with the WHY2-ATLAS tutoring system.

> WHY2-ATLAS: Fine. Using this principle, what is the value of the horizontal component of the acceleration of the egg? Please explain your reasoning.
> Student: zero because there is no horizontal force acting on the egg *[3 propositions expressed]*

Figure 1: Eliciting a one sentence explanation from a student.

> WHY2-ATLAS: Suppose a man is in an elevator that is falling without anything touching it (ignore the air, too). He holds his keys motionless right in front of his face and then just releases his grip on them. What will happen to them? Explain.
>
> Student: *[omitted 15 correct propositions]*... Yet the gravitational pull on the man and the elevator is greater because they are of a greater weight and therefore they will fall faster then the keys. I believe that the keys will float up to the cieling as the elevator continues falling.

Figure 2: An initial elicitation of a multi-sentence explanation from a student.

The only previous tutoring system that has attempted to address longer explanations is AUTOTUTOR (Graesser et al., 2004). It uses a latent semantic

*This research was supported by ONR Grant No. N00014-00-1-0600 and by NSF Grant No. 9720359.

Proceedings of the 3rd Workshop on Scalable Natural Language Understanding, pages 17–24,
New York City, June 2006. ©2006 Association for Computational Linguistics

> *[omitted 16 correct propositions]...* Since <Net force = mass * acceleration> and <F= mass*g> therefore <mass*acceleration= mass*g> and acceleration and gravitational force end up being equal. So mass does not effect anything in this problem and the acceleration of both the keys and the man are the same. *[omitted 46 correct propositions]*...we can say that the keys will remain right in front of the man's face.

Figure 3: A subsequent response from the same student in Figure 2 after some interaction with WHY2-ATLAS.

analysis (LSA) approach where the structure of sentences is not considered. Thus the degree to which details of the explanation are understood is limited.

As can be seen from the examples, a student's explanation about a formal domain such as qualitative physics may involve a number of phenomena: algebraic formulas, NL renderings of formulas, various degrees of formality, and conveying the logical structure of an argument (Makatchev et al., 2005).

Tutoring goals involve eliciting correct statements of the appropriate degree of formality and their justifications to address possible gaps and errors in the explanation. To achieve these goals the NL understanding is required to answer the following questions:

- Does the student explanation contain errors? If yes, what are the likely buggy assumptions that have led the student to these errors?
- What required statements have not been covered by the student? Does the explanation contain statements that are logically close to the required statements?

These requirements imply that a logical structure needs to be imposed on the space of possible domain statements. Considering such a structure to be a model of the student's reasoning about the domain, the two requirements correspond to a solution of a model-based diagnosis problem (Forbus and de Kleer, 1993).

How does one build such a model? A desire to make the process scalable and feasible necessitates an automated procedure. The difficulty is that this automated reasoner has to deal with the NL phenomena that are relevant for our application. In turn, this means that the knowledge representation (KR) would have to be able to express these phenomena (e.g. NL renderings of formulas, various degrees of formality). The reasoner has to account for common reasoning fallacies, have flexible consistency constraints and perform within the tight requirements of a real-time dialogue application.

In this paper, we present a hybrid of symbolic and statistical approaches that attempts to robustly provide a model-based diagnosis of a student's explanation. In the next section, we provide a brief sketch of the KR used in WHY2-ATLAS. Section 3 describes our hybrid approach for analyzing student explanations while section 4 covers our most recent evaluations of the system and its explanation analysis components. Section 5 presents our conclusions along with future directions.

2 Knowledge representation

We selected an order-sorted first-order predicate logic (FOPL) as a base KR for our domain since it is expressive enough to reflect the hierarchy of concepts from the qualitative mechanics ontology (Ploetzner and VanLehn, 1997) and has a straightforward proof theory (Walther, 1987). Following the representation used in the abductive reasoner Tacitus-lite (Thomason et al., 1996), our KR is function-free, does not have quantifiers, Skolem constants or explicit negation. Instead all variables in facts or goals are assumed to be existentially quantified, and all variables in rules are either universally quantified (if they appear in premises) or existentially quantified (if they appear in conclusions only).

Although our KR has no explicit negation, some types of negative statements are represented by using (a) complimentary sorts, for example `constant` and `nonconstant`; (b) the value `nonequal` as a filler of the respective argument of comparison predicates.

Instead of parsing arbitrary algebraic expressions, an equation identifier module attempts shallow parsing of equation candidates and maps them into a finite set of anticipated equation labels (Makatchev et al., 2005).

NL understanding needs to distinguish formal versus informal physics expressions so that the tutoring system can coach on proper use of terminology. Many qualitative mechanics phenomena may be described informally, for example "speed up" instead of "accelerate" and "push" instead of "apply a force." The relevant informal expressions fall into the following categories:

- relative position: "keys are behind (in front of, above, under, close, far from, etc.) man"
- motion: "move slower," "slow down," "moves along a straight line"
- dependency: "horizontal speed will not depend on the force"
- direction: "the force is downward"
- interaction: "the man pushes the keys," "the gravity pulls the keys"

Each of these categories (except for the last one) has a dedicated representation. While representing push and pull expressions via a dedicated predicate seems straightforward, we are still assessing the utility of distinguishing "man pushes the keys" and "man applies a force on the keys" for our tutoring application and currently represent both expressions as a nonzero force applied by the man to the keys.

One of the tutoring objectives of WHY2-ATLAS is to encourage students to provide argumentative support for their conclusions. This requires recognizing and representing the justification-conclusion clauses in student explanations. Recognizing such clauses is a challenging NLP problem due to the issue of quantifier and causality scoping. It is also difficult to achieve a compromise between two competing requirements for a suitable representation. First, the KR should be flexible enough to account for a variable number of justifications. Second, reasoning with the KR should be computationally feasible. We leave representing the logical structure of explanations for future work.

3 Analyzing Student Explanations

When analyzing a student explanation, first an equation identifier tags any physics equations in the student's response and then the explanation is classified to complete the assessment. Explanation classification is done by using either (a) a statistical classifier that maps the explanation directly into a set of known facts, principles and misconceptions, or (b) two competing semantic parsers that each generate an FOPL representation that is then matched against known facts, principles or misconceptions, as well as against pre-computed correct and buggy chains of reasoning. We present the approaches at a high-level in order to focus on how the approaches work when combined and our evaluation results.

3.1 Statistical classifier

RAINBOW is a tool for developing *bag of words* (BOW) text classifiers (McCallum and Nigam, 1998). The classes of interest must first be identified and then a text corpus annotated for example sentences for each class. From this training data a bag of words representation is derived for each class and a number of algorithms can be tried for measuring similarity of a new input segment's BOW representation to each class.

For WHY2-ATLAS, the classes are a subset of nodes in the correct and buggy chains of reasoning. Limiting the number of classes allows us to alleviate the problem of sparseness of training data, but the side-effect is that there are many misclassifications of sentences due to overlap in the classes; that is, words that discriminate between classes are shared by many other classes (Pappuswamy et al., 2005). We alleviate this problem some by aggregating classes and building three tiers of BOW text classifiers that use a kNN measure. By doing so, we obtain a 13% improvement in classification accuracy over a single classifier approach (Pappuswamy et al., 2005). The upper two tiers of classification describe the topic of discussion and the lower tier describes the specific principle or misconception related to the topic and subtopic. The first tier classifier identifies which second tier classifier to use and so on. The third tier then identifies which node (if any) in the chain of reasoning a sentence expresses.

But because the number of classes is limited, BOW has problems dealing with many of the NL phenomena we described earlier. For example, although it can deal with some informal language use (i.e. 'push the container' maps to 'apply force on the container'), it cannot provide accurate syntactic-semantic mappings between informal and formal language on the fly. This is because the informal language use is so varied that it is difficult to capture representative training data in sufficient quantities. Hence, a large portion of student statements either cannot be classified with high confidence or are erroneously classified. We use a post-classification heuristic to try to filter out the latter cases. The filtering heuristic depends on the system's representation language and not on the classification technique. Given a classification of which node in the chain of reasoning the sentence represents, the heuristic estimates whether the node's FOPL representation either over- or under-represents the sentence by matching the root forms of the words in the natural language sentence to the constants in the system's representation language.

For those statements BOW cannot classify or that the heuristic filters out, we attempt classification using an FOPL representation derived from semantic parsing, as described in the next two subsections.

3.2 Converting NL to FOPL

Two competing methods of sentence analysis each generate a FOPL candidate. The two candidates are then passed to a heuristic selection process that chooses the best one (Jordan et al., 2004). The rationale for using competing approaches is that the techniques available vary considerably in accuracy, processing time and whether they tend to be brittle and produce no analysis vs. a partial one. There is also a trade-off between these performance measures and the amount of domain specific setup required for each technique.

The first method, CARMEL, provides combined syntactic and semantic analysis using the LCFlex syntactic parser along with semantic constructor functions (Rosé, 2000). Given a specification of the desired representation language, it then maps the analysis to this language. Then discourse level processing attempts to resolve nominal and temporal anaphora and ellipsis to produce the candidate FOPL representation for a sentence (Jordan and VanLehn, 2002).

The second method, RAPPEL, uses MINIPAR (Lin and Pantel, 2001) to parse the sentence. It then extracts syntactic dependency features from the parse to use in mapping the sentence to its FOPL representation (Jordan et al., 2004). Each predicate in the KR language is assigned a predicate template and a separate classifier is trained for each predicate template. For example, there is a classifier that specializes in predicate instantiations (atoms) involving the velocity predicate and another for instantiations of the acceleration predicate. Classes for each template represent combinations of constants that can fill a predicate template's slots to cover all possible instantiations of that predicate. Each predicate template classifier returns either a nil which indicates that there is no instantiation involving that predicate or a class label that corresponds to an instantiation of that predicate. The candidate FOPL representation for a statement is the union of the output of all the predicate template classifiers.

Finally, either the CARMEL or RAPPEL candidate FOPL output is selected using the same heuristic as for the BOW filtering. The surviving FOPL representation is then assessed for correctness and completeness, as described next.

3.3 Analyzing correctness and completeness

As the final step in analyzing a student's explanation, an assessment of correctness and completeness is performed by matching the FOPL representations of the student's response to nodes of an augmented assumption-based truth maintenance system (ATMS) (Makatchev and VanLehn, 2005).

An ATMS for each physics problem is generated off-line. The ATMS compactly represents the deductive closure of a problem's givens with respect to a set of both good and buggy physics rules. That is, each node in the ATMS corresponds to a proposition that follows from a problem statement. Each anticipated student misconception is treated as an assumption (in the ATMS sense), and all conclusions that follow from it are tagged with a label that includes it as well as any other assumptions needed to derive that conclusion. This labeling allows the ATMS to represent many interwoven deductive closures, each depending on different misconceptions, without inconsistency. The labels allow recovery of how a conclusion was reached. Thus a match with a node containing a buggy assumption indicates the student has a common error or misconception and which error or misconception it is.

The completeness of an explanation is relative to a two-column proof generated by a domain expert. A human creates the proof that is used for checking completeness since it is probably less work for a person to write an acceptable proof than to find one in the ATMS. Part of the proof for the problem in Figure 2 is shown in Figure 4 where facts

Step	Fact	Justification
1	The only force on the keys and the man is the force of gravity	Forces are either contact forces or the gravitational force
...	...	...
12	The keys and the man have the same displacements at all times	<Average velocity = displacement / elapsed time>, so if average velocity and time are the same, so is displacement.
13	The keys and the man have the same initial vertical position	given
14	The keys and the man have the same vertical position at all times	<Displacement = difference in position>, so if the initial positions of two objects are the same and their displacements are the same, then so is their final position
15	The keys stay in front of the man's face at all times	

Figure 4: Part of the proof used in WHY2-ATLAS for the Elevator problem in Figure 2.

appear in the left column and justifications that are physics principles appear in the right column. Justifications are further categorized as vector equations (e.g. <Average velocity = displacement / elapsed time>, in step (12) of the proof), or qualitative rules (e.g. "so if average velocity and time are the same, so is displacement" in step (12)). A two-column proof is represented in the system as a directed graph in which nodes are facts, vector equations, or qualitative rules that have been translated to the FOPL representation language off-line. The edges of the graph represent the inference relations between the premise and conclusion of modus ponens.

Matches of an FOPL input against the ATMS and the two-column proof (we collectively referred to these earlier as the correct and buggy chains of reasoning) do not have to be exact. In addition, further flexibility in the matching process is provided by examining a neighborhood of radius N (in terms of graph distance) from matched nodes in the ATMS to determine whether it contains any of the nodes of the two-column proof. This provides an estimate of the proximity of a student's utterance to the facts that are of interest.

Although matching against the ATMS deductive closure has been implemented, the current version of the system does not yet fully utilize this capability. Instead, the correctness and completeness of explanations is evaluated by flexibly matching the FOPL input against targeted relevant facts, principles and misconceptions in the chains of reasoning, using a radius of 0. This kind of matching is referred to as direct matching in Section 4.2.

4 Evaluations

WHY2-ATLAS, as we've just described it, has been fully implemented and was evaluated in the context of testing the hypothesis that even when content is equivalent, students who engage in more interactive forms of instruction learn more. To test this hypothesis we compared students who received human tutoring with students who read a short text. WHY2-ATLAS and WHY2-AUTOTUTOR provided a third type of condition that served as an interactive form of instruction where the content is better controlled than with human tutoring in that only some subset of the content covered in the text condition can be presented. In all conditions the students had to solve four problems that require multi-sentential explanations, one of which is shown in Figure 2.

In earlier evaluations, we found that overall students learn and learn equally well in all three types of conditions when the content is appropriate to the level of the student (VanLehn et al., 2005), i.e. the learning gains for *human tutoring* and the content controlled text were the same. For the latest evaluation of WHY2-ATLAS, which excluded a human tutoring condition, the learning gains on multiple-choice and essay post-tests were the same as for the other conditions. However, on fill-in-the-blank post-tests, the WHY2-ATLAS students scored higher than the text students (p=0.010; F(1,74)=6.33), and this advantage persisted when the scores were adjusted by factoring out pre-test scores in an ANCOVA (p=0.018; F(1,72)=5.83). Although this difference was in the expected direction, it was not accompanied by similar differences for the other two post-tests.

These learning measures show that, relative to the

text, the two systems' overall performance at selecting content is good. A system could perform worse than the text condition if it too frequently misinterprets multi-sentential answers and skips material covered in the text that a student may need. But since the dialogue strategies in the two systems are different and selected relative to the understanding techniques used, we next need to do a detailed corpus analysis of the language data collected to track successes and failures of understanding and dialogue strategy selection relative to knowledge components in the post-test. Next we will describe some component-level evaluations that focus on the parts of the system we just described.

4.1 Evaluating the Benefit of Combining Single Sentence Approaches

This first component-level evaluation focuses on the benefits of heuristically choosing between the results of BOW, CARMEL and RAPPEL. This particular evaluation used a prior version of the system which used BOW without tiers and hand-crafted pattern-matching rules instead of the ATMS approach to assessment. But this evaluation still reflects the potential benefits of combining single sentence approaches.

We used a test suite of 35 held-out multi-sentence student explanations (235 sentences total) that are annotated for the elicitation topics that are to be discussed with the student. We computed recall (R), precision (P) and false alarm rate (FAR) against the full corpus instead of averaging these measures for each explanation. Since F-measure does not allow error skewing as can be done with ROC areas (Flach, 2003) we instead look for cases of high recall with a low false alarm rate.

The top part of Table 1 compares the baseline of tutoring all possible topics and the individual performances of the three approaches when each is used in isolation from the others. We see that only the statistical approach lowers the false alarm rate but does so by sacrificing recall. The rest are not significantly different from tutoring all topics. The poor performances of CARMEL and RAPPEL is not totally unexpected because there are three potential failure points for these classification approaches; the syntactic analysis, the semantic mapping and the hand-crafted pattern matching rules for assessing correctness and completeness. While the syntactic analysis results for both approaches are good, the semantic mapping and assessment of correctness and completeness are still big challenges. The results of BOW, while better than that of the other two approaches, are clearly not good enough.

Table 1: Performance of NL to FOPL for actions taken in WHY2-ATLAS system.

Approach	R	P	FAR
tutor all topics	1.0	.61	1.0
CARMEL	1.0	.61	1.0
BOW without tiers	.60	.93	.07
RAPPEL	.94	.59	1.0
satisficing heuristic	.67	.80	.26
highest ranked heuristic	.73	.76	.36

The bottom part of Table 1, shows the results of combining the approaches and choosing one output heuristically. The satisficing[1] version of the heuristic checks each output in the order 1) CARMEL 2) BOW 3) RAPPEL, and stops with the first representation that is acceptable according to the filtering heuristic. This heuristic selection process modestly improves recall but at the sacrifice of a higher false alarm rate. The highest ranking heuristic scores each output and selects the best one. It provides the most balanced results of the combined or individual approaches. It provides the largest increase in recall and the false alarm rate is still modest compared to the baseline of tutoring all possible topics. It is clear, that a combined approach has a positive impact.

4.2 Completeness and Correctness Evaluation

The component-level evaluation for completeness and correctness was completed after the student learning evaluation. It focuses on the performance of just the direct matching procedure. Figure 5 shows the results of classifying 62 student utterances for one physics problem with respect to 46 stored statement representations using only direct matching. To generate these results, the data is manually divided into 7 groups based on the quality of the NL

[1]According to Newell & Simon (1972), satisficing is the process by which an individual sets an acceptable level as the final criterion and simply takes the first acceptable move instead of seeking an optimal one.

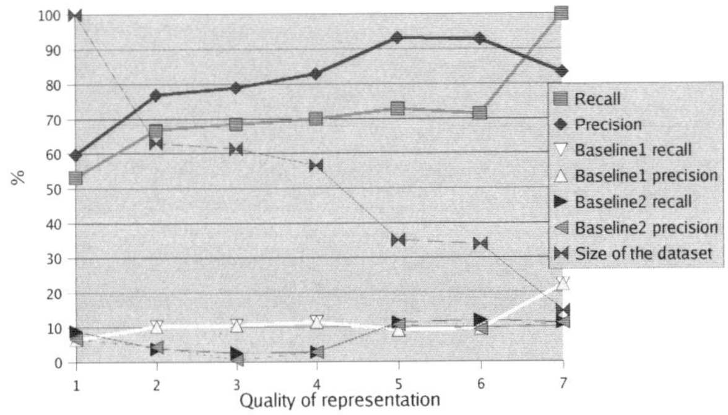

Figure 5: Average recall and precision of utterance classification. The size of a group of entries is shown relative to the size of the overall data set. Average processing time is 0.011 seconds per entry on a 1.8 GHz Pentium 4 machine with 2Gb of RAM.

to FOPL conversion, such that group 7 consists only of perfectly formalized entries, and for $1 \leq n \leq 6$ group n includes entries of group $n+1$ and additionally entries of somewhat lesser representation quality, so that group 1 includes all the entries of the data set. The flexibility of the direct matching algorithm even allows classification of utterances that have mediocre representations, resulting in 70% average recall and 82.9% average precision for 56.5% of all entries (group 4). However, large numbers of inadequately represented utterances (38.7% of all entries did not make it into group 3 of the data set) result in 53.2% average recall and 59.7% average precision for the whole data set (group 1). These results are still significantly better compared to the two baseline classifiers the best of which peaks at 22.2% average recall and precision. The first baseline classifier always assigns the single label that is dominant in the training set (average number of labels per entry of the training set is 1.36). The second baseline classifier independently and randomly picks labels according to their distributions in the training set. The most frequent label in the training set corresponds to the answer to the problem. Since in the test set the answer always appears as a separate utterance (sentence), recall and precision rates for the first baseline classifier are the same.

Although the current evaluation did not involve matching against the ATMS, we did evaluate the time required for such a match in order to make a rough comparison with our earlier approach. Matching a 12 atom input representation against a 128 node ATMS that covers 55% of relevant problem facts takes around 30 seconds, which is a considerable improvement over the 170 seconds required for the on-the-fly analysis performed by the Tacitus-lite+ abductive reasoner (Makatchev et al., 2004)—the technique used in the previous version of WHY2-ATLAS. The matching is done by a version of a largest common subgraph-based graph-matching algorithm (due to the need to account for cross-referencing atoms via shared variables) proposed in (Shearer et al., 2001), that has a time complexity $O(2^n n^3)$, where n is the size of an input graph. The efficiency can be further improved by using an approximation of the largest common subgraph in order to evaluate the match.

5 Conclusion

In this paper, we discussed an application that integrates a hybrid of semantic parsers and a symbolic reasoner with a statistical classifier to analyze student explanations. We attempted to address the problem that the leap made by statistical classifiers from NL to a feasible classification is too big since too many details of what was actually said by the student are lost. On the other hand, we showed that the hybrid semantic parsers allow for a slightly smaller leap by mapping to a symbolic representation that is sufficient for domain reasoning. Using deductive closure of problem givens and buggy assumptions, the correctness and completeness analyzer allows us to reason about the correctness of student statements that cannot be confidently classified statistically. Although formal and informal language expressions have unique underlying semantics, we attempt to paraphrase informal NL into formal NL by using the forward-chaining rules involved in creating the deductive closure for a problem from its givens. Our current symbolic representation is still too coarse to distinguish some fine nuances allowed by the domain of mechanics. We conjecture that extending our knowledge representation with more language-specific predicates would allow us to represent more fine-grained differences in student statements while still allowing feasible reasoning with the ATMS.

References

Michelene T. H. Chi, Stephanie A. Siler, Heisawn Jeong, Takashi Yamauchi, and Robert G. Hausmann. 2001. Learning from human tutoring. *Cognitive Science*, 25(4):471–533.

M. Evens and J. Michael. 2006. *One-on-One Tutoring by Humans and Computers*. Lawrence Erlbaum Associates, Inc.

P. Flach. 2003. The geometry of ROC space: Understanding machine learning metrics through ROC isometrics. In *Proceedings of 20th International Conference on Machine Learning*.

Kenneth D. Forbus and Johan de Kleer. 1993. *Building Problem Solvers*. MIT Press, Cambridge, Massachusetts; London, England.

A.C. Graesser, S. Lu, G.T. Jackson, H. Mitchell, M. Ventura, A. Olney, and M.M. Louwerse. 2004. Autotutor: A tutor with dialogue in natural language. *Behavioral Research Methods, Instruments, and Computers*, 36:180–193.

W. Lewis Johnson and Jeff Rickel. 1997. Steve: An animated pedagogical agent for procedural training in virtual environments. *SIGART Bulletin*, pages 16–21, Fall.

Pamela Jordan and Kurt VanLehn. 2002. Discourse processing for explanatory essays in tutorial applications. In *Proceedings of the 3rd SIGdial Workshop on Discourse and Dialogue*, July.

Pamela W. Jordan, Maxim Makatchev, and Kurt VanLehn. 2004. Combining competing language understanding approaches in an intelligent tutoring system. In *Proceedings of the Intelligent Tutoring Systems Conference*.

D. Lin and P. Pantel. 2001. Discovery of inference rules for question answering. *Journal of Natural Language Engineering*, 7(4):343–360.

Maxim Makatchev and Kurt VanLehn. 2005. Analyzing completeness and correctness of utterances using an ATMS. In *Proceedings of Int. Conference on Artificial Intelligence in Education, AIED2005*. IOS Press, July.

Maxim Makatchev, Pamela W. Jordan, and Kurt VanLehn. 2004. Abductive theorem proving for analyzing student explanations to guide feedback in intelligent tutoring systems. *Journal of Automated Reasoning, Special issue on Automated Reasoning and Theorem Proving in Education*, 32:187–226.

Maxim Makatchev, Brian S. Hall, Pamela W. Jordan, Umarani Pappuswamy, and Kurt VanLehn. 2005. Mixed language processing in the Why2-Atlas tutoring system. In *Proceedings of the Workshop on Mixed Language Explanations in Learning Environments, AIED2005*, pages 35–42, July.

Andrew McCallum and Kamal Nigam. 1998. A comparison of event models for naive bayes text classifi cation. In *Proceeding of AAAI/ICML-98 Workshop on Learning for Text Categorization*. AAAI Press.

A. Newell and H.A. Simon. 1972. *Human Problem Solving*. Prentice-Hall, Englewood Cliffs, NJ.

Umarani Pappuswamy, Dumisizwe Bhembe, Pamela W. Jordan, and Kurt VanLehn. 2005. A multi-tier NL-knowledge clustering for classifying students' essays. In *Proceedings of 18th International FLAIRS Conference*.

S. Peters, E. Bratt, B. Clark, H. Pon-Barry, and K. Schultz. 2004. Intelligent systems for training damage control assistants. In *In the Proceedings of I/ITSEC 2004*, Orlando, Florida.

Rolf Ploetzner and Kurt VanLehn. 1997. The acquisition of qualitative physics knowledge during textbook-based physics training. *Cognition and Instruction*, 15(2):169–205.

Carolyn Rosé, Pamela Jordan, Michael Ringenberg, Stephanie Siler, Kurt VanLehn, and Anders Weinstein. 2001. Interactive conceptual tutoring in atlas-andes. In *Proceedings of AI in Education 2001 Conference*.

Carolyn P. Rosé. 2000. A framework for robust semantic interpretation. In *Proceedings of the First Meeting of the North American Chapter of the Association for Computational Linguistics*, pages 311–318.

Kim Shearer, Horst Bunke, and Svetha Venkatesh. 2001. Video indexing and similarity retrieval by largest common subgraph detection using decision trees. *Pattern Recognition*, 34(5):1075–1091.

Richmond H. Thomason, Jerry Hobbs, and Johanna D. Moore. 1996. Communicative goals. In K. Jokinen, M. Maybury, M. Zock, and I. Zukerman, editors, *Proceedings of the ECAI 96 Workshop Gaps and Bridges: New Directions in Planning and Natural Language Generation*.

K. VanLehn, A. Graesser, G. T. Jackson, P. Jordan, A. Olney, and C. P. Rosé. 2005. When is reading just as effective as one-on-one interactive human tutoring? In *Proceedings of CogSci2005*.

Christof Walther. 1987. *A many-sorted calculus based on resolution and paramodulation*. Morgan Kaufmann, Los Altos, California.

Claus Zinn, Johanna D. Moore, and Mark G. Core. 2002. A 3-tier planning architecture for managing tutorial dialogue. In *Proceedings of Intelligent Tutoring Systems Conference (ITS 2002)*, pages 574–584.

Increasing the coverage of a domain independent dialogue lexicon with VERBNET

Benoit Crabbé*, **Myroslava O. Dzikovska***, **William de Beaumont**†, **Mary Swift**†
* ICCS-HCRC, University of Edinburgh, 2 Buccleuch Place, EH8 9LW, Edinburgh, UK
{bcrabbe,mdzikovs}@inf.ed.ac.uk
†Department of Computer Science, University of Rochester, Rochester NY, USA
{wdebeaum,swift}@cs.rochester.edu

Abstract

This paper investigates how to extend coverage of a domain independent lexicon tailored for natural language understanding. We introduce two algorithms for adding lexical entries from VERBNET to the lexicon of the TRIPS spoken dialogue system. We report results on the efficiency of the method, discussing in particular precision versus coverage issues and implications for mapping to other lexical databases.

1 Introduction

This paper explores how different lexicons can be integrated with the goal of extending coverage of a deep parser and semantic interpreter. Lexical semantic databases (Kipper et al., 2000; Johnson and Fillmore, 2000; Dorr, 1997) use a frame-based model of lexical semantics. Each database groups words in classes where predicative words and their arguments are described. The classes are generally organised in an inheritance structure. Each such database can be used, among other things, to perform semantic interpretation. However, their actual structures are quite different, reflecting different underlying methodological approaches to lexical description, and this results in representation that are not directly compatible. Since no such database has full coverage of English, it is worth combining them in order to get a lexicon with better coverage and a unified representation for English.

We explore the issues related to merging verb descriptions from two lexical databases, which have both syntactic and semantic incompatibilities, and compare two techniques for aligning semantic classes and the syntax-semantics mappings between them. The resulting lexicon is to be used in precise interpretation tasks, so its consistency and accuracy are a high priority. Thus, though it is possible to generate lexical entries automatically (Kwon and Hovy, 2006; Swift, 2005), we use a semi-automatic method in which an expert hand-checks the automatically generated entries before adding them to the lexicon. Therefore, our goal is to maximise the number of new useful entries added to the lexicon while minimising the number of entries that are discarded or hand-edited.

We take the mapping between the TRIPS lexicon and the VERBNET lexical database as a case study for our experiment. The TRIPS lexicon is used together with a parser to provide a natural language understanding component for several dialogue applications in different domains. It outputs highly detailed semantic representations suitable for complex dialogue tasks such as problem-solving and tutoring dialogue, *inter alia*. An essential feature of TRIPS is the integration of a detailed lexical semantic representation, semantic classes and theta role assignments in the parsing process.

Semantic types and role labelling are helpful in both deep (Tetreault, 2005) and shallow interpretation tasks (Narayanan and Harabagiu, 2004). TRIPS provides a convenient test case because its grammar is already equipped with the formal devices required to build up a frame-based semantic representation including this information.[1]

[1]While wide coverage grammars such as the *English Re-*

Proceedings of the 3rd Workshop on Scalable Natural Language Understanding, pages 25–32,
New York City, June 2006.

We chose VERBNET to extend the TRIPS lexicon because it includes a detailed syntax-semantic mappings, thus providing a more convenient interface to the syntactic component of the grammar than lexicons where this connection is left unclear, such as FRAMENET. However the methods described here are designed to be reusable for merging other lexical databases, in particular we intend to experiment with FRAMENET in the near future.

The plan of the paper is as follows: we first describe the target lexicon (Section 2) and the source lexicon (Section 3) for our experiment before describing the methodology for integration (Section 4). We finally present an evaluation of the techniques in Section 5.

2 The TRIPS Lexicon

The TRIPS lexicon (Dzikovska, 2004) is the target of the mapping procedure we describe in Section 4. It includes syntactic and semantic information necessary to build semantic representations usable in dialogue systems. The TRIPS parser is equipped with a fairly detailed grammar, but a major restriction on coverage in new domains is often lack of lexical information. The lexicon used in our evaluation comprised approximately 700 verb lemmas with 1010 senses (out of approximately 2500 total word senses, covering both open- and closed-class words). The lexicon is designed for incremental growth, since the lexical representation is domain-independent and the added words are then re-used in new domains.

A graphical representation of the information stored in the TRIPS lexicon and used in parsing is shown in Figure 1. The lexicon is a list of canonical word entries each of which is made of a set of sense definitions comprised of a LF type and a syntax-semantic template.

Semantic classes (LF types) in the TRIPS lexicon are organised in a domain-independent ontology (the LF ontology). The LF Ontology was originally based on a simplified version of FRAMENET

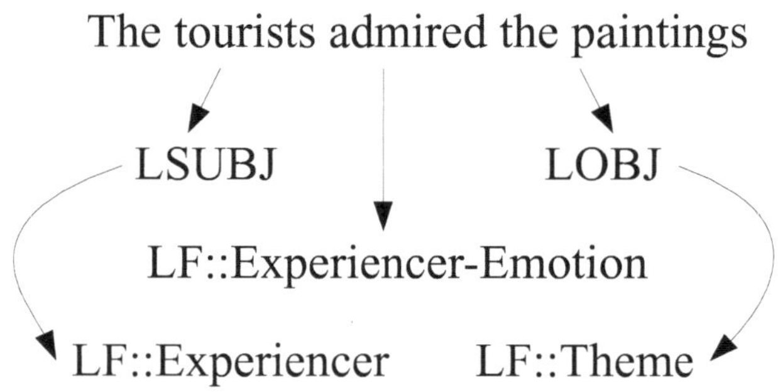

Figure 1: Information in the TRIPS word sense definition for mapping between syntactic and semantic roles.

(Baker et al., 1998; Dzikovska et al., 2004), with each LF type describing a particular situation, object or event and its participants. *Syntax-Semantics Templates* (or templates) capture the linking between the syntax and semantics (LF type and semantic roles) of a word. The semantic properties of an argument are described by means of a semantic role assigned to it and selectional restrictions.[2]

The TRIPS grammar contains a set of independently described lexical rules, such as the passive or dative shift rules, which are designed to create non-canonical lexical entries automatically, while preserving the linking properties defined in the canonical entry.

In this context adding an entry to the lexicon requires determining both the list of LF types and the list of templates for canonical contexts, that is, the list of mappings between a logical frame and a canonical subcategorization frame.

3 VERBNET

VERBNET (Kipper et al., 2000) provides an actual implementation of the descriptive work carried out by Levin (1993), which has been extended to cover prepositional constructions and corpus-based subcategorization frames (Kipper et al., 2004; Kipper et al., 2006).

VERBNET is a hierarchical verb lexicon in which verbs are organised in classes. The fundamental assumption underlying the classification is that the members of a given class share a similar syntactic

source Grammar (Copestake and Flickinger, 2000) build deep semantic representations which account for scoping and temporal structure, their lexicons do not provide information related to word senses and role labels, in part due to the additional difficulty involved building a wide coverage lexicon with the necessary lexical semantic information.

[2]The selectional restrictions are domain independent and specified using features derived from EuroWordNet (Vossen, 1997; Dzikovska et al., to appear).

behaviour, that is, they pattern in the same set of alternations, and are further assumed to share common semantic properties.[3]

VERBNET classes are organised in an inheritance hierarchy. Each class includes a set of members (verbs), a set of (subcategorization) frames and a set of semantic descriptions. Frames are descriptions of the linking between syntax and semantics for that class. Each frame argument contains a syntactic category augmented with syntactic features, and a corresponding thematic role. Each class also specifies a set of additional selectional restriction features. VERBNET further includes for each class a semantic description stated in terms of event semantics, that we ignore in this paper.

4 Methodology

The methodology used in the mapping process consists of two steps. First we translate the source, VERBNET, to an intermediate representation best suited for parsing purposes. Second this intermediate representation is translated to a specific target, here the TRIPS lexicon. At this stage of our work, the translation from VERBNET to the intermediate representation mainly concerns normalising syntactic information coded in VERBNET to make them easier to handle for parsing purposes, and the translation from the intermediate representation to the TRIPS lexicon focuses on translating semantic information. This architecture is best understood as a cross compilation scheme: we further expect to reuse this intermediate representation for producing outputs for different parsers and to accept inputs from other lexical databases such as FRAMENET.

4.1 The intermediate representation

The intermediate representation is a lexical representation scheme mainly tailored for parsing: in this context, a lexicon is thus made of a set of words, each of which consists of a lemma, a syntactic category and a list of sense definitions. Each sense definition has a name and a frame. The name of the sense definition is actually the name of the VERBNET class it derives from. The frame of the sense definition has a list of arguments, each of which consists of a syntactic category, a syntactic function, a thematic role and possibly a set of prepositions and syntactic feature structures.

The content of the intermediate representation uses the following data categories. Syntactic categories, thematic roles and features are those used in VERBNET. We further add the syntactic functions described in (Carroll et al., 1998). Specifically, two categories left implicit in VERBNET by the use of feature structures are made explicit here: prepositional phrases (PP) and sentential arguments (S).

Each argument described in a sense definition frame is marked with respect to its coreness status. The coreness status aims to provide the lexicon with an operational account for common discrepancies between syntax and semantics descriptions. This status may be valued as *core, non-core* or *non-sem* and reflects the status of the argument with respect to the syntax-semantics interface.

Indeed, there is a methodological pitfall concerning the mapping between thematic roles and syntactic arguments: semantic arguments are not defined following criteria identical to those for syntactic arguments. The main criterion for describing semantic arguments is their participation in the event, situation, object described by the frame whereas the criterion for describing syntactic arguments is based on the obligatoriness or the specificity of the argument with respect to the verb. The following example illustrates such conflicts:

(1) a. It is raining

b. I am walking to the store

The *It* in example (1a) plays no role in the semantic representation, but is obligatory in syntax since it fills a subject position. The locative PP in example (1b) is traditionally not treated as an argument in syntax, rather as a modifier, hence it does not fill a complement position. Such phrases are, however, classified in VERBNET as part of the frames. Following this, we distinguish three kinds of arguments: *non-sem* as in (1a) are syntactic-only arguments with no semantic contribution. *non-core* as in (1b) contribute to the semantics but are not subcategorized.

[3] In practice, it turns out that there are exceptions to that hypothesis (Kipper, 2005).

4.2 From VERBNET to the intermediate representation

Given VERBNET as described in Section 3 and the intermediate representation we described above, the translation process requires mainly (1) to turn the class based representation of VERBNET into a list-of-word based representation (2) to mark arguments for coreness (3) to merge some arguments and (4) to annotate arguments with syntactic functions.

The first step is quite straightforward. Every member m of every VERBNET class C is associated with every frame of C yielding a new sense definition in the intermediate representation for m.

In the second step, each argument receives a coreness mark. Arguments marked as *non-core* are adverbs, and prepositional phrases introduced by a large class of prepositions (e.g. spatial prepositions). The arguments marked as *non-sem* are those with an impersonal *it*, typically members of the *weather* class. All other arguments listed in VERBNET frames are marked as *core*.

In the third step, syntactic arguments are merged to correspond better to phrase-based syntax.[4] For example, the VERBNET encoding of subcategorization frames splits prepositional frames on two slots: one for the preposition and one for the noun phrase. We have merged the two arguments, to become a PP, also merging their syntactic and semantic features. Other merges at this stage include merging possessive arguments such as *John's brother* which are described with three argument slots in VERBNET frames. We merged them as a single NP.

The last step in the translation is the inference of syntactic functions. It is possible to reasonably infer syntactic functions from positional arguments and syntactic categories by (a) considering the following oblicity order over the set of syntactic functions used in the intermediate representation:[5]

(2) NCSUBJ < DOBJ < OBJ2 < {IOBJ, XCOMP,CCOMP}

[4]We also relabel some categories for convenience without affecting the process. For instance, VERBNET labels both clausal arguments and noun phrases with the category NP. The difference is made with syntactic features. We take advantage of the features to relabel clausal arguments with the category S.

[5]This order is partial, such that the 3 last functions are unordered wrt to each other. These functions are the subset of the functions described in (Carroll et al., 1998) relevant for handling VERBNET data.

and by (b) considering this problem as a transduction problem over two tapes. One tape being the tape of syntactic categories and the second the tape of syntactic functions. Given that, we designed a transducer that implements a category to function mapping. It implements the above oblicity order together with an additional mapping constraint: nouns can only map to NCSUBJ, DOBJ, prepositional phrases can only map to OBJ2, IOBJ, infinitival clauses can only map to XCOMP and finite clauses to CCOMP.

We further added refinements to account for frames that do not encode their arguments following the canonical oblicity order: for dealing with dative shift encoded in VERBNET with two different frames and for dealing with impersonal contexts, so that we eventually used the transducer in Figure 2. All states except 0 are meant to be final. The transduction operates only on *core* and *non-sem* arguments, *non-core* arguments are systematically associated with an adjunct function. This transducer is capable of correctly handling the majority of VERBNET frames, finding a functional assignment for more than 99% of the instances.

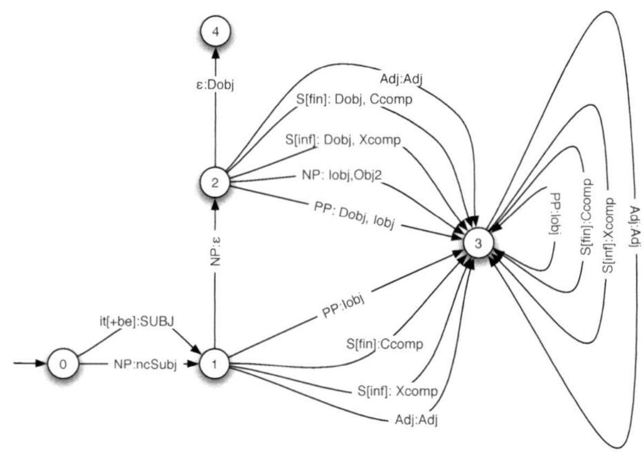

Figure 2: A transducer for assigning syntactic functions to ordered subcategorization frames

4.3 From Intermediate representation to TRIPS

Recall that a TRIPS lexical entry is comprised of an LF type with a set of semantic roles and a template representing the mappings from syntactic functions to semantic roles. Converting from our intermediate representation to the TRIPS format involves two steps:

- For every word sense, determine the appropriate TRIPS LF type

- Establish the correspondence between VERBNET and TRIPS syntactic and semantic arguments, and generate the appropriate mapping in the TRIPS format.

We investigated two strategies to align semantic classes (VERBNET classes and TRIPS LFs). Both use a class intersection algorithm as a basis for decision: two semantic classes are considered a match if they are associated with the same lexical items.

The intersection algorithm takes advantage of the fact that both VERBNET and TRIPS contain lexical sets. A lexical set for VERBNET is a class name and the set of its members, for TRIPS it is an LF type and the set of words that are associated with it in the lexicon. Our intersection algorithm computes the intersection between every VERBNET lexical set and every TRIPS lexical set. The sets which intersect are then considered as candidate mappings from a VERBNET class to a TRIPS class.

However, this technique produces many 1-word class intersections, and leads to spurious entries. We considered two ways of improving precision: first by requiring a significantly large intersection, second by using syntactic structure as a filter. We discuss them in turn.

4.4 Direct Mapping Between Semantic Representations

The first technique which we tried for mapping between TRIPS and VERBNET semantic representations is to map the classes directly. We consider all candidate mappings between the TRIPS and VERBNET classes, and take the match with the largest intersection. We then align the semantic roles between the two classes and produce all possible syntax-semantics mappings specified by VERBNET. This technique has the advantage of providing the most complete set of syntactic frames and syntax-semantics mappings which can be retrieved from VERBNET. However, since VERBNET lists many possible subcategorization frames for every word, guessing the class incorrectly is very expensive, resulting in many spurious senses generated. We use a class intersection threshold to improve reliability.

VERBNET ROLE	TRIPS ROLES
Theme	LF::THEME, LF::ADDRESSEE, LF::ALONG, LF::ENTITY
Cause	LF::CAUSE, LF::THEME
Experiencer	LF::EXPERIENCER, LF::COGNIZER
Source	LF::FROM-LOC, LF::SOURCE, LF::PATH
Destination	LF::GOAL, LF::TO-LOC
Recipient	LF::RECIPIENT, LF::ADDRESSEE, LF::GOAL
Instrument	LF::INSTRUMENT

Table 1: Sample VERBNET to TRIPS role mappings

At present, we count an LF type match as successfully guessed if there is an intersection in lexical entries above the threshold (we determined 3 words as a best value by finding an optimal balance of precision/recall figures over a small gold-standard mapping set). Since the classes contain closely related items, larger intersection means a more reliable mapping. If the VERBNET class is not successfully mapped to an LF type then no TRIPS lexical entry is generated.

Once the correspondence between the LF type and the VERBNET class has been established, semantic arguments have to be aligned between the two classes. We established a role mapping table (a sample is shown in Table 1), which is an extended version of the mapping from Swift (2005). The role mapping is one to many (each VERBNET role maps to 1 to 8 TRIPS roles), however, since the appropriate LF type has been identified prior to argument mapping, we usually have a unique mapping based on the roles defined by the LF type.[6]

Once the classes and semantic roles have been aligned, the mapping of syntactic functions between the intermediate representation and TRIPS syntax is quite straightforward. Functional and category mappings are one to one and do not raise specific problems. Syntactic features are also translated into TRIPS representation.

To illustrate the results obtained by the automatic mapping process, two of the sense definitions generated for the verb *relish* are shown in Figure 3. The TRIPS entries contain references to the class description in the TRIPS LF ontology (line introduced by

[6] In rare cases where more than 1 correspondence is possible, we are using the first value in the intersection as the default.

```
;; entries
(relish
  (SENSES
   ((EXAMPLE "The tourists admired the paintings")
    (LF-PARENT LF::EXPERIENCER-EMOTION)
    (TEMPL VN-EXPERIENCER-THEME-TEMPL-84))
   ((EXAMPLE "The children liked that the clown had a red nose")
    (LF-PARENT LF::EXPERIENCER-EMOTION)
    (TEMPL VN-EXPERIENCER-THEME-XP-TEMPL-87))
    ))
;;Templates
(VN-EXPERIENCER-THEME-TEMPL-84
 (ARGUMENTS
  (LSUBJ (% NP) LF::EXPERIENCER)
  (LOBJ (% NP) LF::THEME)
  ))
(VN-EXPERIENCER-THEME-XP-TEMPL-87
 (ARGUMENTS
  (LSUBJ (% NP) LF::EXPERIENCER)
  (LCOMP (% CP (vform fin) (ctype s-finite)) LF::THEME)
  ))
```

Figure 3: Sample TRIPS generated entries

LF-PARENT) and to a template (line introduced by TEMPL) generated on the fly by our syntactic conversion algorithm. The first sense definition and template in Figure 3 represent the same information shown graphically in Figure 1. Each argument in a template is assigned a syntactic function, a feature structure describing its syntactic properties, and a mapping to a semantic role defined in the LF type definition (not depicted here).

4.5 Filtering with syntactic structure

The approach described in the previous section provides a fairly complete set of subcategorization frames for each word, provided that the class correspondence has been established successfully. However, it misses classes with small intersections and classes for which some but not all members match (see Section 5 for discussion). To address these issues we tried another approach that automatically generates all possible class matches between TRIPS and VERBNET, again using class member intersection, but using the a TRIPS syntactic template as an additional filter on the class match. For each potential match, a human evaluator is presented with the following:

```
{confidence score
{verbs in TRIPS-VN class intersection}/
LF-type TRIPS-template
 => VN-class: {VN class members}}
```

The confidence score is based on the number of verbs in the intersection, weighted by taking into account the number of verbs remaining in the respective TRIPS and VERBNET classes. The template used for filtering is taken from all templates that occur with the TRIPS words in this intersection (one match per template is generated for inspection). For example:

```
93.271%
{clutch,grip,clasp,hold,wield,grasp}/
lf::body-manipulation agent-theme-xp-templ
 => hold-15.1-1: {handle}
```

This gives the evaluator additional syntactic information to make the judgement on class intersections. The evaluator can reject entire class matches, or just individual verbs from the VERBNET class which don't quite fit an otherwise good match. We only used the templates already in TRIPS (those corresponding to each of the word senses in the intersection) to avoid overwhelming the evaluator with a large number of possibly spurious template matches resulting from an incorrect class match. This technique allows us to pick up class matches based on a single member intersection, such as:

```
7.814%
{swallow}/
lf::consume agent-theme-xp-templ
=> gobble-39.3-2: {gulp,guzzle,quaff,swig}
```

However, the entries obtained are not guaranteed to cover all frames in VERBNET because if a given alternation is not already covered in TRIPS, it is not derived from VERBNET with this method.

5 Evaluation and discussion

Since our goal in this evaluation is to balance the coverage of VERBNET with precision, we correspondingly evaluate along those two dimensions. For both techniques, we evaluate how many word senses were added, and the number of different words defined and VERBNET classes covered. As a measure of precision we use, for those entries which were retrieved, the percentage of those which could be taken "as is" (good entries) and the percentage of entries which could be taken with minor edits (for example, changing an LF type to a more specific subclass, or changing a semantic role in a template). The results of evaluation are shown in Table 2.[7]

Since for mapping with syntax filtering we considered all possible TRIPS-VERBNET intersections, it in effect presents an upper bound the number of words shared between the two databases. Further

[7] "nocos" table rows exclude the other_cos VERBNET class, which is exceptionally broad and skews evaluation results.

	Class mapping					Mapping with syntax filtering				
Type	Total	Good	Edit	Bad	%usable	Total	Good	Edit	Bad	%usable
Sense	3075	1000	196	1879	0.39	11036	1688	87	9261	0.16
Word	744	274	98	372	0.5	2138	1211	153	714	0.64
Class	15	10	1	4	0.73	198	129	2	67	0.66
Sense-nocos	1136	654	196	286	0.75	7989	1493	87	6409	0.20
Word-nocos	422	218	98	106	0.75	1763	1059	153	491	0.69
Class-nocos	14	9	1	4	0.71	197	128	2	67	0.65

Table 2: Evaluation results for different acquisition techniques. %usable = (good + editable) / bad".

extension would require extending the TRIPS LF Ontology with additional types to cover the missing classes. As can be seen from this table, 65% of VERBNET classes have an analogous class in TRIPS. At the same time, there is a very large number of class intersections possible, so if all possible intersections are generated, only a very small percentage of generated word senses (16%) is usable in the combined system. Thus developing techniques to filter out the irrelevant senses and class matches is important for successful hand-checking.

Our evaluation also shows that while class intersection with thresholding provides higher precision, it does not capture many words and verb senses. One reason for this is data sparsity. TRIPS is relatively small, and both TRIPS and VERBNET contain a number of 1-word classes, which cannot be reliably mapped without human intervention. This problem can be alleviated in part as the size of the database grows. We expect this technique to have better recall when the combined lexicon is used to merge with a different lexical database such as FRAMENET.

However, a more difficult issue to resolve is differences in class structure. VERBNET was built around the theory of syntactic alternations, while TRIPS used FRAMENET structure as a starting point, simplifying the role structure to make connection to parsing more straightforward (Dzikovska et al., 2004). Therefore TRIPS does not require that all words associated with the same LF type share syntactic behaviour, so there are a number of VERBNET classes with members which have to be split between different TRIPS classes based on additional semantic properties. 70% of all good matches in the filtering technique were such partial matches. This significantly disadvantages the thresholding technique, which provides the mappings on class level, not allowing for splitting word entries between the classes.

We believe that the best solution can be found by combining these two techniques. The thresholding technique could be used to establish reliable class mappings, providing classes where many entries could be transferred "as is". The mapping can then be examined to determine incorrect class mappings as well as the cases where classes should be split based on individual words. For those entries judged reliable in the first pass, the syntactic structure can be transferred fully and quickly, while the syntactic filtering technique, which requires more manual checking, can be used to transfer other entries in the intersections where class mapping could not be established reliably.

Establishing class and member correspondence is a general problem with merging any two semantic lexicons. Similar issues have been noted in comparing FRAMENET and VERBNET (Baker and Ruppenhofer, 2002). A method recently proposed by Kwon and Hovy (2006) aligns words in different semantic lexicons to WordNet senses, and then aligns semantic roles based on those matches. Since we are designing a lexicon for semantic interpretation, it is important for us that all words should be associated with frames in a shared hierarchy, to be used in further interpretation tasks. We are considering using this alignment technique to further align semantic classes, in order to produce a shared database for interpretation covering words from multiple sources.

6 Conclusion

In this paper, we presented a methodology for merging lexicons including syntactic and lexical semantic information. We developed a model based on cross-compilation ideas to provide an intermediate representation which could be used to generate entries for different parsing formalisms. Mapping semantic properties is the most difficult part of the process, and we evaluated two different techniques for establishing correspondence between classes and lexical entries, using TRIPS and VERBNET lexicons as a case study. We showed that a thresholding technique has a high precision, but low recall due to inconsistencies in semantic structure, and data sparsity. We can increase recall by partitioning class intersections more finely by filtering with syntactic structure. Further refining the mapping technique, and using it to add mappings to other lexical databases such as FRAMENET is part of our ongoing work.

Acknowledgements

We thank Karin Kipper for providing us useful documentation on the VERBNET feature system, and Charles Callaway for technical help with the final version. This material is based on work supported by grants from the Office of Naval Research under numbers N000140510048 and N000140510043, from NSF #IIS-0328811, DARPA #NBCHD030010 via subcontract to SRI #03-000223 and NSF #E1A-0080124.

References

C. F. Baker and J. Ruppenhofer. 2002. Framenet's frames vs. Levin's verb classes. In *Proceedings of the 28th Annual Meeting of the Berkeley Linguistics Society*, pages 27–38.

C. F. Baker, C. Fillmore, and J. B. Lowe. 1998. The Berkeley Framenet project. In *Proceedings of CoLing-ACL*, Montreal.

J. Carroll, E. Briscoe, and A. Sanfilippo. 1998. Parser evaluation: A survey and a new proposal. In *Proceedings of LREC-98*.

A. Copestake and D. Flickinger. 2000. An open source grammar development environment and broad-coverage English grammar using HPSG. In *Proceedings of LREC-2000*, Athens, Greece.

B. Dorr. 1997. Large-scale dictionary construction for foreign language tutoring and interlingual machine translation. *Machine Translation*, 12(4):271–375.

M. O. Dzikovska, M. D. Swift, and J. F. Allen. 2004. Building a computational lexicon and ontology with FrameNet. In *Proceedings of LREC workshop on Building Lexical Resources from Semantically Annotated Corpora*, Lisbon.

M. O. Dzikovska, M. D. Swift, and J. F. Allen. to appear. Customizing meaning: Building domain-specific semantic representations from a generic lexicon. In H. Bunt, editor, *Computing Meaning, Volume 3*, Studies in Linguistics and Philosophy. Kluwer.

M. O. Dzikovska. 2004. *A Practical Semantic Representation for Natural Language Parsing*. Ph.D. thesis, University of Rochester, Rochester NY.

C. Johnson and C. J. Fillmore. 2000. The FrameNet tagset for frame-semantic and syntactic coding of predicate-argument structure. In *Proceedings ANLP-NAACL 2000*, Seattle, WA.

K. Kipper, H. T. Dang, and M. Palmer. 2000. Class-based construction of a verb lexicon. In *Proceedings of AAAI*, Austin.

K. Kipper, B. Snyder, and M. Palmer. 2004. Using prepositions to extend a verb lexicon. In *Proceedings of HLT-NAACL 2004 Workshop on Computational Lexical Semantics*, pages 23–29, Boston, MA.

K. Kipper, A. Korhonen, N. Ryant, and M. Palmer. 2006. Extending Verbnet with novel verb classes. In *Proceedings of LREC-2006*.

K. Kipper. 2005. *Verbnet: A broad coverage, comprehensive verb lexicon*. Ph.D. thesis, University of Pennsylvania.

N. Kwon and E. H. Hovy. 2006. Integrating semantic frames from multiple sources. In A. F. Gelbukh, editor, *CICLing*, volume 3878 of *Lecture Notes in Computer Science*, pages 1–12. Springer.

B. Levin. 1993. *English Verb Classes and Alternations*. The University of Chicago Press.

S. Narayanan and S. Harabagiu. 2004. Question answering based on semantic structures. In *Proceedings of International Conference on Computational Linguistics (COLING 2004)*, Geneva, Switzerland.

M. Swift. 2005. Towards automatic verb acquisition from Verbnet for spoken dialog processing. In *Proceedings of Interdisciplinary Workshop on the Identification and Representation of Verb Features and Verb Classes*, Saarbruecken, Germany.

J. Tetreault. 2005. *Empirical Evaluations of Pronoun Resolution*. Ph.D. thesis, University of Rochester.

P. Vossen. 1997. Eurowordnet: A multilingual database for information retrieval. In *Proceedings of the Delos workshop on Cross-language Information Retrieval*.

Scaling Natural Language Understanding via User-driven Ontology Learning

Berenike Loos
European Media Laboratory, GmbH
Schloss-Wolfsbrunnenweg 33, 69118 Heidelberg, Germany
firstname.lastname@eml-d.villa-bosch.de

Abstract

Non-statistical natural language understanding components need world knowledge of the domain for which they are applied in a machine-readable form. This knowledge can be represented by manually created ontologies. However, as soon as new concepts, instances or relations are involved in the domain, the manually created ontology lacks necessary information, i.e. it becomes obsolete and/or incomplete. This means its "world model" will be insufficient to understand the user. The scalability of a natural language understanding system, therefore, essentially depends on its capability to be up to date. The approach presented herein applies the information provided by the user in a dialog system to acquire the knowledge needed to understand him or her adequately. Furthermore, it takes the position that the type of incremental ontology learning as proposed herein constitutes a viable approach to enhance the scalability of natural language systems.

1 Introduction

To let a computer system understand natural language one needs knowledge about objects and their relations in the real world. As the manual modeling and maintenance of such knowledge structures, i.e. ontologies, are not only time and cost consuming, but also lead to not-scalable systems, there exists a demand to build and populate them automatically or at least semi automatically. This is possible by analyzing unstructured, semi-structured or fully structured data by various linguistic as well as statistical means and by converting the results into an ontological form.

In an open-domain scalable natural language understanding (NLU) system the automatic learning of ontological concepts and corresponding relations between them is essential, as a complete modeling of the world is neither practicable nor feasible, as the real world and its objects, models and processes are constantly changing along with their denotations.

This paper assumes that a viable approach to this challenging problem is to learn ontological concepts and relations relevant to a certain user in a given context by the dialog system at the time of the user's inquiry. My central hypothesis is that the information about terms that lack any mapping to the employed knowledge representation of the language understanding component can only be found in topical corpora such as the Web. With the help of this information one can find the right node in the ontology to append the concept corresponding to the unknown term in case it is a noun or to insert it as an instance in case it is a proper noun or another named entity.

The goal of the ontology learning component is to extend the knowledge base of the NLU system and therefore it will gradually adapt to the user's needs.

An example from the area of spoken dialog systems would be that of a user walking through the city of Heidelberg and asking: "How do I get to

Proceedings of the 3rd Workshop on Scalable Natural Language Understanding, pages 33–40,
New York City, June 2006.

the Auerstein". This would lead to the detection of *Auerstein* as being neither recognizable by the speech recognizer nor mappable to the knowledge representation of the system. Therefore, the corresponding hypernym of *Auerstein* has to be found on the internet by recourse to additional information about the context of the user. In this case, the additional information consists of the location of the user, namely *Heidelberg*. Once found, the hypernym is mapped to a corresponding concept, which already exists in the ontology. If there is no such corresponding concept, the concept for the hypernym thereof has to be determined. The formerly unknown term is mapped to a concept and is integrated into the system's ontology as a child of the concept for the found hypernym. In case the unknown term is a proper noun, it is integrated as an instance of the concept for the hypernym. So far, the research undertaken is related to nouns and proper nouns, also more generally referred to as *terms* in this paper.

In the following section, I will describe related work undertaken to solve the task of ontology learning, followed by some remarks of the distinction between ontology learning and natural language in Section 3. Thereafter, I will sketch out the minimal stages involved in the type of ontology learning proposed herein in Section 4.

2 Related Work

The capability to acquire knowledge exactly at the time it is needed can be regarded as an important stepping stone towards scalable natural language understanding systems. The necessity of scalability in NLU became more and more obvious in open-domain dialog systems, as the knowledge base integrated into those can never be complete. Before the emergence of open-domain systems, more or less complete ontologies were modeled manually for the domain needed in the NLU system and were therefore not scalable to additional domains, unless modeled in advance in a manual fashion or by means of off-line ontology learning. Nonetheless, numerous off-line ontology learning frameworks exist, which alleviate the work of an ontology engineer to construct knowledge manually (Maedche, 2002), (Schutz and Buitelaar, 2005), (Cimiano et al., 2005). Most of these frameworks apply hybrid methods to optimize their learning results.

For example, the ontology population method OntoLearn (Navigli et al., 2004) is based on text mining and other machine learning techniques and starts with a generic ontology like WordNet and documents in a given domain. The result is a domain extended and trimmed version of the initial ontology. For this, the system applies three phases to learn concepts:

- First, a terminology extraction method, using shallow techniques that range from stochastic methods to more sophisticated syntactic approaches, is applied, which extracts a list of domain terms (mostly nouns and proper nouns) from a set of documents representative for a given domain.
- Second, a semantic interpretation takes place which makes use of a compositional interpretation and structural semantic interconnections.
- After these two phases the extending and trimming of the initial ontology takes place. With the help of the semantic interpretation of the terms they can be organized in sub-trees and appended under the appropriate node of the initial ontology applying linguistic rules.

The text understanding system SYNDICATE (SYNthesis of DIstributed Knowledge Acquired from Texts) uses an integrated ontology learning module (Hahn and Marko, 2002). In this approach new concepts are learned with the help of text understanding, which applies two different sources of evidence, namely, the prior knowledge of the topic domain of the texts and grammatical constructions in which unknown lexical items occur in the texts.

In an incremental process a given ontology is updated as new concepts are acquired from real-world texts. The acquisition process is centered on the linguistic and conceptual "quality" of various forms of evidence underlying the generation and refinement of concept hypotheses. On the basis of the quality of evidence, concept hypotheses are ranked according to credibility and the most credible ones are selected for assimilation into the domain knowledge base.

The project Disciple (Stanescu et al., 2003) builds agents which can be initially trained by a subject matter expert and a knowledge engineer, in a way similar to how an expert would teach an apprentice. A Disciple agent applies two different methods for ontology learning, i.e. exception-based and example-based ontology learning. The exception-based learning approach consists of four main phases:

- First, a candidate discovery takes place, in which the agent analyzes a rule together with its examples, exceptions and the ontology and finds the most plausible types of extensions of the latter that may reduce or eliminate the rule's exceptions.

- In the second phase the expert interacts with the agent to select one of the proposed candidates.

- Afterwards the agent elicits the ontology extension knowledge from the expert and finally a rule refinement takes place, in which the agent updates the rule and eliminates its exceptions based on the performed ontology extension.

- When the subject matter expert has to specify a fact involving a new instance or new feature in the agent teaching process, the example-based learning method is invoked. In this process the agent tries to find example sentences of the words next to a new term through various heuristics. For instance, he finds out that X is member of Y, and consequently can ask the expert. If he affirms, the new term can be memorized.

All of the approaches described above exhibit theoretical as well as practical (in the light of the task undertaken herein) shortcomings. The theoretical problems that have not been resolved in a satisfactory manner by the works described above (as well as numerous others) are:

- a clear separation of the linguistic and ontological subtasks involved in the overall ontology learning endeavor

- systematic ways and methods for evaluating the individual learning results

- rigorously defined baselines against which to evaluate the ensuing learning approaches.

In the following I will describe how these issues can be addressed within the user-driven ontology learning framework proposed herein.

3 Natural Language versus Ontology Learning

Before describing the actual ontology learning process it is important to make a clear distinction between the two fields involved: This is on the one hand natural language and on the other hand ontology learning.

The corpora to extract knowledge from should come from the internet as this source provides the most up-to-date information. The natural language texts are rich in terms, which can be used as labels of concepts in the ontology and rich in semantic relations, which can be used as ontological relations (aka properties).

The connection between the two areas which are working on similar topics but are using different terminology needs a distinction between the extraction of semantic information from natural language and the final process of integrating this knowledge into an ontology.

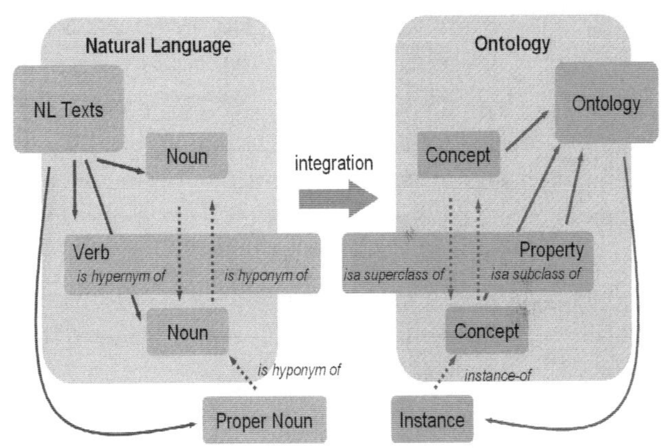

Figure 1: Natural Language versus Ontology Learning

Figure 1 shows the process of ontology learning from natural language text. On the left side relevant natural language terms are extracted. During a transformation process they are converted into labels of concepts and relations of an ontology. Proper nouns are transfered into instance labels in the ontology[1].

[1] In our understanding the term *ontology* denotes both the instance model as well as the ground ontology.

4 Scaling NLU via User-driven Ontology Learning

A user-driven ontology learning framework should be able to acquire knowledge at the run time of the NLU system. Therefore, terms which are not understood by the system have to be identified. In dialog systems this is true for all terms uttered or written by a user, which are not presently contained in the lexicon or can be derived by means of derivational or flexional morphology. In the following I will refer to these terms as *unknown terms*[2].

When a user of an open-domain spoken dialog system makes an utterance, it happens regularly, that the term is not represented in the system's lexicon. Since it is assumed, in this work, that the meaning of terms is represented by means of a formal ontology, a user-driven ontology learning framework is needed to determine the corresponding concepts for these terms, e.g., via a search on topical corpora. For instance, a term such as *Auerstein* could be employed to query a search engine. By applying natural language patterns, as proposed by Hearst (1992) and statistical methods, as proposed by Faulhaber et al. (2006) possible hypernyms or sets of hypernym candidates of the term can be extracted. For these a corresponding concept (or set of possible concepts) in the ontology employed by the dialog system need to be found. Last but not least the unknown term has to be inserted into the ontology as either an instance or a subclass of that concept. This process is described in greater detail in Section 5.4).

It is important to point out that terms often have more than one meaning, which can only be determined by recourse to the context in which it is uttered/found (Widdows, 2003), (Porzel et al., 2006). Therefore, information about this context needs to be added in order to make searching for the right hypernym feasible[3] as shown in Section 5.3. For example, the term *Lotus* can refer to a flower, a specific type of car or among copious other real world entities to a restaurant in Heidelberg. Therefore, a scalable ontology learning framework in a dialog system requires at least the following ingredients:

[2]This closely corresponds to what is termed *out-of-vocabulary (OOV) words* in the automatic speech recognition community.

[3]Of course, even in the same context a term can have more than one meaning as discussed in Section 5.7.

- A formal explicit model of a shared conceptualization of a specific domain of interest (Gruber, 1993), i.e. an ontology;
- processing methods which indicate the unknown terms;
- a corpus, as the starting point to retrieve hypernyms;
- methods for mapping hypernyms to concepts in the ontology;
- an evaluation framework;

Figure 2 shows the steps involved in on-demand ontology learning from the text to the knowledge side.

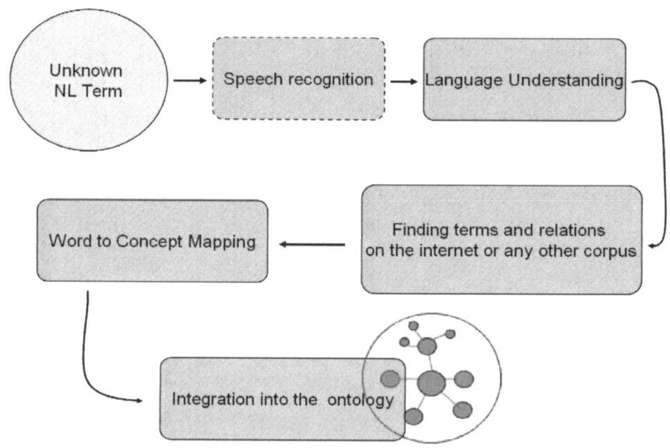

Figure 2: From text to knowledge

5 On-demand learning

From the cognitive point of view learning makes only sense when it happens on-demand. On-demand means, that it occurs on purpose and that activity is involved rather than passivity. As pointed out by Spitzer (2002) for human beings activity is necessary for learning. We cannot learn by drumming data into our brain through listening cassettes when sleeping or by similar fruitless techniques. The reason for this is, that we need active ways of structuring the data input into our brain. Furthermore, we try only to learn what we need to learn and are therefore quite economic with the "storage space" in our brain.

It makes not only for humans sense to simply learn whatever they need and what is useful for them. Therefore, I propose that ontology learning, as any other learning, is only useful and, in the end, possible if it is situated and motivated by the given context and the user needs. This can entail learning missing concepts relevant to a domain or to learn new concepts and instances which become necessary due to changes in a domain.

However, the fundamental ontological commitments should be adhered to. So, for example, the decision between a revisionary and a descriptive ontology should be kept in the hand of the knowledge engineer, as well as the choice between a multiplicative and a reductionist modeling[4]. As soon as the basic structure is given new knowledge can be integrated into this structure. Thus, for a reductionist ontology a concept such as *Hotel* should be appended only once, e.g. to an ontological concept as *PhysicalObject* rather than *NonPhysicalObject*.

In the following I will describe the various steps and components involved in on-demand ontology learning.

5.1 Unknown terms in dialog systems

In case the dialog system works with spoken language one can use the out-of-vocabulary (OOV) classification of the speech recognizer about all terms not found in the lexicon (Klakow et al., 2004). A solution for a phoneme-based recognition is the establishment of corresponding best-rated grapheme-chain hypotheses (Gallwitz, 2002). Those can be used for a search on the internet. In case the dialog system only works with written language it is easier to identify terms, which cannot be mapped to ontological concepts, at least if they are spelled correctly. To evaluate the framework itself adequately it is useful to apply only correctly written terms for a search.

Later on in both cases - i.e. in spoken and written dialog systems - a ranking algorithm of the best, say three, hypotheses should be selected to find the most adequate term. Here methods like the one of Google "Did you mean..." for spelling errors could be used.

[4]More information on these and other ontological choices can be found summarized in (Cimiano et al., 2004)

5.2 Language Understanding

All correctly recognized terms of the user utterance can be mapped to concepts with the help of an analysis component. Frequently, production systems (Engel, 2002), semantic chunkers (Bryant, 2004) or simple word-to-concept lexica (Gurevych et al., 2003) are employed for this task. Such lexica assign corresponding natural language terms to all concepts of an ontology. This is especially important for a later semantic disambiguation of the unknown term (Loos and Porzel, 2004). In case the information of the concepts of the other terms of the utterance can help to evaluate results: When there is more than one concept proposal for an instance (i.e. on the linguistic side a proper noun like *Auerstein*) found in the word-to-concept lexicon, the semantic distance between each proposed concept and the other concepts of the user's question can be calculated[5].

5.3 Linguistic and Extra-linguistic Context

Not only linguistic but also extra linguistic context plays an important role in dialog systems. Thus, to understand the user in an open-domain dialog system it is important to know the extra-linguistic context of the utterances. If there is a context module or component in the system it can give information on the discourse domain, time and location of the user. This information can be used as a support for a search on the internet. E.g. the location of the user when searching for, say *Auerstein*, is advantageous, as in the context of the city *Heidelberg* it has a different meaning than in the context of another city (Bunt, 2000), (Porzel et al., 2006).

Part of the context information can be represented by the ontology as well as patterns for grouping a number of objects, processes and parameters for one distinctive context (Loos and Porzel, 2005).

5.4 Finding the appropriate hypernym on the internet

For this, the unknown term as well as an appropriate context term (if available) needs to be applied for searching possible hypernyms on the Web. As mentioned before an example could be the unknown term *Auerstein* and the context term *Heidelberg*.

[5]E.g. with the single-source shortest path algorithm of Dijkstra (Cormen et al., 2001).

For searching the internet different encyclopedias and search engines can be used and the corresponding results can be compared. After a distinction between different types of unknown terms, the search methods are described.

Global versus local unknown terms: In the case of generally familiar proper nouns like stars, hotel chains or movies (so to say global unknown terms), a search on a topical encyclopedia can be quite successful. In the case of proper nouns, only common in a certain country region, such as Auerstein (Restaurant), Bierbrezel (Pub) and Lux (Cinema), which are local unknown terms, a search in an encyclopedia is generally not fruitful. Therefore, one can search with the help of a search engine.

As one can not know the kind of unknown terms beforehand, the encyclopedia search should be executed before the one using the search engine. If no results are produced, the latter will deliver them (hopefully). In case results are retrieved by the former, the latter can still be used to test those.

Encyclopedia Search: The structure of Encyclopedia entries is generally pre-assigned. That means, a program can know, where to find the most suitable information beforehand. In the case of finding hypernyms the first sentence in the encyclopedia description is often found to be the most useful. To give an example from Wikipedia[6], here is the first sentence for the search entry ***Michael Ballack***:

(1) *Michael Ballack* (born September 26, 1976 in Grlitz, then East Germany) IS A German **football player**.

With the help of lexico-syntactic patterns, the hypernym can be extracted. These so-called Hearst patterns (Hearst, 1992) can be expected to occur frequently in lexicons for describing a term. In example 1 the pattern *X is a Y* would be matched and the hypernym *football player* of the term *Michael Ballack* could be extracted.

Title Search: To search only in the titles of web pages might have the advantage, that results can be generated relatively fast. This is important as real-time performance is an important usability factor in dialog systems. When the titles contain the hypernym it still is to be expected that they might not consist of full sentences, Hearst patterns (Hearst, 1992) are, therefore, unlikely to be found. Alternatively, only the nouns in the title could be extracted and their occurrences counted. The noun most frequently found in all the titles could then be regarded as the most semantically connected term. To aid such frequency-based approaches stemming and clustering algorithms can be applied to group similar terms.

Page Search: For a page search Hearst patterns as in the encyclopedia search can almost certainly be applied. In contrast to encyclopedia entries the recall of those patterns is not so high in the texts from the web pages.

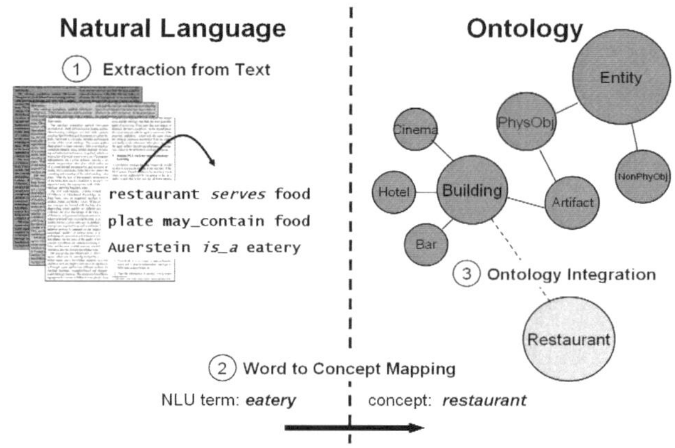

Figure 3: Tasks for the evaluation of ontology learning

The text surrounding the unknown term is searched for nouns. Equal to the title search the occurrence of nouns can then be counted. With the help of machine learning algorithms a text mining can be done to ameliorate the results.

5.5 Mapping text to knowledge by term narrowing and widening

As soon as an appropriate hypernym is found in a text the corresponding concept name should be determined. For term narrowing, the term has to be stemmed to its most general form. For the term widening, this form is used to find synonyms. Those

[6]Wikipedia is a free encyclopedia, which is editable on the internet: http://www.wikipedia.org (last access: 26th January 2006).

are, in turn, used for searching ontological concept names in the ontology integration phase. If the hypernym found is in a language other than the one used for the ontology, a translation of the terms has to take place as well.

5.6 Integration into an ontology

After the mapping phase newly learned concepts, instances or relations can be integrated into any domain-independent or even foundational ontology. If no corresponding concept can be found the next more general concept has to be determined by the techniques described above.

5.7 Evaluation

An evaluation of such a system can be divided into two types: one for the performance of the algorithms before the deployment of the system and one, which can be performed by a user during the run time of the system.

Methodological evaluation Before integrating the framework into a dialog system or any other NLU system an evaluation of the methods and their results should take place. Therefore, a representative baseline has to be established and a *gold-standard* (Grefenstette, 1994) created, depending on the task which is in the target of the evaluation. The ensuing steps in this type of evaluation are shown in Figure 3 and described here in their order:

1. The extraction of hypernyms of unknown words from text and the extraction of semantic relations (other than *is-a*) between NLU terms.

2. The mapping of a linguistic term to an ontological concept.

3. The integration of ontological concepts, instances and relations into the system's ontology.

Depending on the three steps the most adequate baseline method or algorithm for each of them has to be identified. In step 1 for the extraction of hypernyms a chance baseline as well as a majority class baseline will not do the job, because their performance would be too poor. Therefore, a well established algorithm which, for example applies a set of standard Hearst patterns (Hearst, 1992) would constitute a potential candidate. For the mapping from text to knowledge (see step 2) the baseline could be a established by standard stemming combined with string similarity metrics. In case of different source and goal languages an additional machine translation step would also become necessary. For the baseline of ontology evaluation a task-based framework as proposed by (Porzel and Malaka, 2005) could be employable.

Evaluation by the user As soon as the framework is integrated into a dialog system the only way to evaluate it is by enabling the user to browse the ontological additions at his or her leisure and to decide whether terms have been understood correctly or not. In case two or more hypernyms are scored with the same – or quite similar – weights, this approach could also be quite helpful. An obvious reason for this circumstance is, that the term in question has more than one meaning in the same context. Here, only a further inquiry to the user can help to disambiguate the unknown term. In the *Auerstein* example a question like "Did you mean the hotel or the restaurant?" could be posed. Even though the system would show the user that it did not perfectly understand him/her, the user might be more contributory and less annoyed than with a question like "What did you mean?". The former question could also be posed by a person familiar with the place, to disambiguate the question of someone in search for *Auerstein* and would therefore mirror a human-human dialogs, which in turn would furthermore lead to more natural human-computer dialogs.

6 Concluding Remarks

In this paper I have shown, that the scalability of non-statistical natural language understanding systems essentially depends on its capability to be up to date when it comes to understand language. Furthermore, I took the position that ontology learning is viable, when it happens incrementally and in a context-sensitive fashion. Future work will focus on implementation and evaluation within a running multi-modal dialog system. Additionally, a tight integration with automatic lexicon and grammar learning is of paramount importance.

References

John Bryant. 2004. Scalable construction-based parsing and semantic analysis. In *Proceedings of the 2nd International Workshop on Scalable Natural Language Understanding (ScaNaLU 2004) at HLT-NAACL 2004*.

Harry Bunt. 2000. Dialogue pragmatics and context specification. In H.C. Bunt and W.J. Black, editors, *Computational Pragmatics, Abduction, Belief and Context; Studies in Computational Pragmatics*, pages 81–150. John Benjamins, Amsterdam.

Philipp Cimiano, Andreas Eberhart, Daniel Hitzler, Pascal Oberle, Steffen Staab, and Rudi Studer. 2004. The SmartWeb foundational ontology. *SmartWeb Project Report*.

Philipp Cimiano, Günter Ladwig, and Steffen Staab. 2005. Gimme' the context: Context-driven automatic semantic annotation with C-PANKOW. In *Proceedings of the 14th World Wide Web Conference*. ACM Press.

Thomas H. Cormen, Charles E. Leiserson, Ronald L. Rivest, and Clifford Stein. 2001. Section 24.3: Dijkstra's algorithm. In *Introduction to Algorithms, Second Edition*, pages 595–601. MIT Press and McGraw-Hill.

Ralf Engel. 2002. SPIN: Language understanding for spoken dialogue systems using a production system approach. In *Proceedings of the International Conference on Speech and Language Processing 2002*, Denver, USA.

Arndt Faulhaber, Berenike Loos, Robert Porzel, and Rainer Malaka. 2006. Open-class named entity classification in multiple domains. In *Proceedings of the Ontolex Workshop*. Genua, Italy.

Florian Gallwitz. 2002. *Integrated Stochastic Models for Spontaneous Speech Recognition*. Logos, Berlin.

Gregory Grefenstette. 1994. *Explorations in Automatic Thesaurus Discovery*. Kluwer Academic Publishers, USA.

Thomas Gruber. 1993. A translation approach to portable ontology specifications. *Knowledge Acquisition (5)*.

Iryna Gurevych, Rainer Malaka, Robert Porzel, and Hans-Peter Zorn. 2003. Semantic coherence scoring using an ontology. In *Proc. of the HLT/NAACL 2003*, page (in press), Edmonton, CN.

Udo Hahn and Kornl G. Marko. 2002. Ontology and lexicon evolution by text understanding. In *Proceedings of the ECAI 2002 Workshop on Machine Learning and Natural Language Processing for Ontology Engineering (OLT'2002)*. Lyon, France.

Marti A. Hearst. 1992. Automatic acquisition of hyponyms from large text corpora. In *Proceedings of COLING 92*, Nantes, France.

Dietrich Klakow, Georg Rose, and Xavier Aubert. 2004. Oov-detection in a large vocabulary system using automatically defined word-fragments as filler. In *Proceedings of EUROSPEECH'99*, Budapest, Hungary.

Berenike Loos and Robert Porzel. 2004. Resolution of lexical ambiguities in spoken dialogue systems. In *Proceedings of the 5th Workshop on Diascourse and Dialogue*, Cambridge, Massachusetts, USA.

Berenike Loos and Robert Porzel. 2005. Towards ontology-based pragmatic analysis. In *Proceedings of DIALOR'05*, Nancy, France.

Alexander Maedche. 2002. *Ontology Learning for the Semantic Web*. Kluwer Academic Publishers, USA.

Roberto Navigli, Paola Velardi, Alessandro Cucchiarelli, and Francesca Neri. 2004. Extending and enriching WordNet with OntoLearn. In *Proceeedings of Integrated Approach for Web Ontology Learning and Engineering*. IEEE Computer.

Robert Porzel and Rainer Malaka. 2005. A task-based framework for ontology learning, population and evaluation. *Ontology Learning from Text: Methods, Evaluation and Applications Frontiers in Artificial Intelligence and Applications Series*, 123.

Robert Porzel, Iryna Gurevych, and Rainer Malaka. 2006. In context: Integrating domain- and situation-specific knowledge. *SmartKom Foundations of Multimodal Dialogue Systems, Springer, Cognitive Technologies*.

Alexander Schutz and Paul Buitelaar. 2005. RelExt: A tool for relation extraction in ontology extension. In *Proceedings of the 4th International Semantic Web Conference*. Galway, Ireland.

Manfred Spitzer. 2002. *Lernen*. Spektrum Akademischer Verlag.

Bogdan Stanescu, Cristina Boicu, Gabriel Balan, Marcel Barbulescu, Mihai Boicu, and Gheorghe Tecuci. 2003. Ontologies for learning agents: Problems, solutions and directions. In *Proceedings of the 2003 IEEE International Conference on Systems, Man and Cybernetics, Volume: 3*. Washington D.C.

Dominic Widdows. 2003. A mathematical model for context and word-meaning. In *International and Interdisciplinary Conference on Modeling and Using Context*. Stanford, California.

Catching Metaphors

Matt Gedigian, John Bryant, Srini Narayanan, and **Branimir Ciric**
International Computer Science Institute
1947 Center Street. Suite 600
Berkeley, CA 94704, USA
{gedigian, jbryant, snarayan}@icsi.berkeley.edu

Abstract

Metaphors are ubiquitous in language and developing methods to identify and deal with metaphors is an open problem in Natural Language Processing (NLP). In this paper we describe results from using a maximum entropy (ME) classifier to identify metaphors. Using the Wall Street Journal (WSJ) corpus, we annotated all the verbal targets associated with a set of frames which includes frames of spatial motion, manipulation, and health. One surprising finding was that over **90%** of annotated targets from these frames are used metaphorically, underscoring the importance of processing figurative language. We then used this labeled data and each verbal target's PropBank annotation to train a maximum entropy classifier to make this literal vs. metaphoric distinction. Using the classifier, we reduce the final error in the test set by 5% over the verb-specific majority class baseline and 31% over the corpus-wide majority class baseline.

1 Introduction

To move beyond "factoid" style questions, question answering systems must rely on inferential mechanisms. To answer such commonplace questions as *Which train should I take to get to the airport?* requires justifications, predictions and recommendations that can only be produced through inference.

One such question answering system (Narayanan and Harabagiu, 2004) takes PropBank/FrameNet annotations as input, uses the PropBank targets to indicate which actions are being described with which arguments and produces an answer using probabilistic models of actions as the tools of inference. Initiating these action models is called *simulation*.

Such action models provide deep inferential capabilities for embodied domains. They can also, when provided with appropriate metaphoric mappings, be extended to cover metaphoric language (Narayanan, 1997). Exploiting the inferential capabilities of such action models over the broadest domain requires a system to determine whether a verb is being used literally or metaphorically. Such a system could then activate the necessary metaphoric mappings and initiate the appropriate simulation.

2 Metaphor

Work in Cognitive Semantics (Lakoff and Johnson, 1980; Johnson, 1987; Langacker, 1987; Lakoff, 1994) suggests that the structure of abstract actions (such as *states*, *causes*, *purposes*, and *means*) are characterized cognitively in terms of *image schemas* which are *schematized* recurring patterns from the embodied domains of force, motion, and space.

Consider our conceptualization of events as exemplified in the mapping called the Event Structure Metaphor.

- States are locations (bounded regions in space).
- Changes are movements (into or out of bounded regions).

Proceedings of the 3rd Workshop on Scalable Natural Language Understanding, pages 41–48,
New York City, June 2006.

- Causes are forces.
- Actions are self-propelled movements.
- Purposes are destinations.
- Difficulties are impediments to motion.

This mapping generalizes over an extremely wide range of expressions for one or more aspects of event structure. For example, take states and changes. We speak of *being in* or *out of* a state, of *entering* or *leaving* it, of *getting to a state* or *emerging from* it. This is a rich and complex metaphor whose parts interact in complex ways. To get an idea of how it works, consider the submapping Difficulties are impediments to motion. In the metaphor, purposeful action is self-propelled motion toward a destination. A difficulty is something that impedes such motion. Metaphorical difficulties of this sort come in five types: blockages; features of the terrain; burdens; counterforces; lack of an energy source. Here are examples of each: Blockages: *He's trying to get around the regulations. We've got him boxed into a corner.* Features of the terrain: *It's been uphill all the way. We've been hacking our way through a jungle of regulations.* Burdens: *He's carrying quite a load. Get off my back!* Counterforces: *Quit pushing me around. She's leading him around by the nose.* Lack of an energy source: *I'm out of gas. We're running out of steam.*

In summary, these metaphors are ontological mappings across conceptual domains, from the source domain of motion and forces to the target domain of abstract actions. The mapping is conventional, that is, it is a fixed part of our conceptual system, one of our conventional ways of conceptualizing actions. Conventional metaphors capture generalizations governing polysemy, over inference patterns, and governing novel metaphorical language (Lakoff and Turner, 1989).

2.1 Metaphors vs. Different Word Senses

Presumably, one could treat the metaphoric usage of *run* as a different sense, much in the same way that *move forward on a business plan* is treated as a different sense from literal *move forward*. From a parsing/information extraction point of view, these two approaches are equivalent in terms of their representational requirements.

The benefit of employing the metaphor-based approach, as suggested in the introduction, comes when performing inference. As shown by (Narayanan, 1997), a metaphorical usage and a literal usage share inferential structure. For example, the aspectual structure of *run* is the same in either domain whether it is literal or metaphorical usage. Further, this sharing of inferential structure between the source and target domains simplifies the representational mechanisms used for inference making it easier to build the world models necessary for knowledge-intensive tasks like question answering (Sinha and Narayanan, 2005).

3 Objective

While this work in Cognitive Semantics is suggestive, without a corpus-based analysis, it is hard to accurately estimate the importance of metaphoric information for Natural Language Processing (NLP) tasks such as Question Answering or Information Distillation. Our work is a first step to remedy this situation. We start with our computational definition of metaphor as a mapping from concrete to abstract domains. We then investigate the Wall Street Journal (WSJ) corpus, selecting a subset of its verbal targets and labeling them as either metaphoric or literal. While we had anticipated the pervasiveness of metaphor, we could not anticipate just how pervasive with over 90% of the labeled data being metaphoric.

Provided with labeled training data, our task is to automatically classify the verbal targets of unseen utterances as either metaphoric or literal. Motivated by the intuition that the types of a target's arguments are important for making this determination, we extracted information about the arguments from the PropBank (Kingsbury et al., 2002) annotation for each sentence, using WordNet (Fellbaum, 1998) as the type hierarchy.

3.1 Using Verbal Arguments

A metaphor is a structured mapping between the roles of two frames that makes it possible to describe a (usually) more abstract concept in terms of a more concrete one (Lakoff and Johnson, 1980). The more abstract concept is referred to as the *target* domain while the more concrete concept is referred to as the

1. MET : Texas Air has {run} into difficulty...
2. LIT : "I was doing the laundry and nearly broke my neck {running} upstairs to see ...

Figure 1: Examples taken from the WSJ Corpus. MET indicates a metaphoric use of the target verb and LIT indicates a literal use.

source domain. More precisely, the metaphor maps roles of the target frame onto the source frame.

Figure 1 shows some example sentences with a particular verbal target *run* in curly braces. Example 1 is a *metaphoric* usage (marked by MET) of *run* where the *destination* role is filled by the state of *difficulty*. Example 2 is a *literal* usage (marked by LIT) of *run*.

The arguments of a verb are an important factor for determining whether that verb is being used metaphorically. If they come from the source domain frame, then the likelihood is high that the verb is being used literally. In the example literal sentence from Figure 1, the theme is a person, which is a physical object and thus part of the source domain.

If, on the other hand, the arguments come from the target domain, then it is likely that the verb is being used metaphorically. Consider the metaphorical *run* from Figure 1. In that case, both the theme and the goal of the action are from the target domain. Thus any approach that tries to classify sentences as literal or metaphoric must somehow incorporate information about verbal arguments.

4 Data

Because no available corpus is labeled for the metaphoric/literal distinction, we labeled a subset of the WSJ corpus for our experiments. To focus the task, we concentrated on motion-related frames that act as the source domain for the Event Structure Metaphor and some additional non-motion based frames including *Cure* and *Placing*. Figure 2 shows the selected frames along with example lexical units from each frame.

To identify relevant sentences we first obtained from FrameNet a list of lexical units that evoke the selected source frames. Since WSJ is labeled with PropBank word senses, we then had to determine which PropBank senses correspond to these

Frame	Example LUs
Motion	*float, glide, go, soar*
Motion-directional	*drop, fall, plummet*
Self-motion	*amble, crawl, hobble*
Cause-motion	*catapult, haul, throw, yank*
Cotheme	*accompany, escort, pursue*
Placing	*cram, heap, pocket, tuck*
Cure	*cure, ease, heal, treat*

Figure 2: The frames selected for annotation and some of the lexical units that evoke them.

Cure Frame LU	PropBank Sense
alleviate	alleviate.01
cure	cure.01
ease	ease.02
heal	heal.01
rehabilitate	rehabilitate.01
resuscitate	resuscitate.01
treat	treat.03

Figure 3: The lexical units that evoke the *Cure* frame and each unit's associated PropBank sense[2].

FrameNet lexical items. The lexical items that evoke the *Cure* frame and the corresponding PropBank senses are shown in Figure 3.

As anyone who has inspected both PropBank and FrameNet can attest, these two important lexical resources have chosen different ways to describe verbal senses and thus in many cases, determining which PropBank sense corresponds to a particular FrameNet sense is not a straightforward process. Verbs like *slide* have a single PropBank sense used to describe both the *slid* in *The book slid off the table* and the *slid* in *I slid the book off the table.* While FrameNet puts *slide* both in the *Motion* frame and in the *Cause-motion* frame, PropBank uses the argument labeling to distinguish these two senses.

Periodically, PropBank has two senses, one for the literal interpretation and one for the metaphoric interpretation, where FrameNet uses a single sense. Consider the word *hobble* and its two senses in PropBank:

- hobble.01 "walk as if feet tied together"
- hobble.02 "tie the feet of, metaphorically 'hinder'"

Frame	#MET	#LIT	Total	%MET
Cause-motion	461	44	505	91
Cotheme	926	8	934	99
Motion-directional	1087	21	1108	98
Placing	888	110	998	89
Self-motion	424	86	510	83
Cure	105	26	131	80
All_Frames	3891	295	4186	93

Figure 4: The number of targets annotated metaphoric or literal, broken down by frame.

Lexical Unit	#MET	#LIT
alleviate	8	0
cure	7	3
ease	81	0
heal	3	0
rehabilitate	1	0
resuscitate	2	0
treat	3	23

Figure 5: The lexical units that evoke the *Cure* frame and each unit's counts for metaphoric (#MET) and literal (#LIT) usage.

Because we intended to classify both literal and metaphoric language, both PropBank senses of *hobble* were included. However most verbs do not have distinct literal and metaphoric senses in PropBank.

The final step in obtaining the relevant portion of the WSJ corpus is to use the lists of PropBank senses that corresponding to the FrameNet frames and extract sentences with these targets. Because the PropBank annotations label which PropBank sense is being annotated, this process is straightforward.

Having obtained the WSJ sentences with items that evoke the selected source frames, we labeled the data using a three-way split:

- MET: indicating metaphoric use of the target
- LIT: indicating literal use of the target
- ? : indicating a target that the annotator was unsure of

For our experiments, we concentrated only on those cases where the label was MET or LIT and ignored the unclear cases.

As is shown in Figure 4, the WSJ data is heavily weighted towards metaphor over all the frames that we annotated. This tremendous bias towards metaphoric usage of motion/cause-motion lexical items shows just how prevalent the Event Structure Metaphor is, especially in the domain of economics where it is used to describe market fluctuations and policy decisions.

Figure 5 shows the breakdown for each lexical item in the *Cure* frame. Note that most of the frequently occurring verbs are strongly biased towards either a literal or metaphoric usage. *Ease*, for example, in all 81 of its uses describes the easing of an economic condition and not the easing of pain. *Treat* on the other hand, is overwhelmingly biased towards the treating of physical and psychological disorders and is only rarely used for an abstract disorder.

5 The Approach

As has been discussed in this paper, there are at least two factors that are useful in determining whether the verbal target of an utterance is being used metaphorically:

1. The bias of the verb
2. The arguments of the verbal target in that utterance

To determine whether the arguments suggest a metaphoric or a literal interpretation, the system needs access to information about which constituents of the utterance correspond to the arguments of the verbal target. The PropBank annotations fill this role in our system. For each utterance that is used for training or needs to be classified, the gold standard PropBank annotation is used to determine the verbal target's arguments.

For every verbal target in question, we used the following method to extract the types of its arguments:

1. Used PropBank to extract the target's arguments.
2. For each argument, we extracted its head using rules closely based on (Collins, 1999).

Feature Schema	Example Instantiation	Comment
verb	*verb=treat*	The verbal target
ARG0_TYPE	uninstantiated	ARG0 (Doctor role) not present
ARG1_TYPE	uninstantiated	ARG1 (Patient role) not present
ARG2_TYPE	*ARG2_TYPE=anemia*	The WordNet type is *anemia*.
ARG3_TYPE	*ARG3_TYPE=drug*	The WordNet type is *drug*.

Figure 6: The feature schemas used for classification. The instantiated features are drawn from the sentence *The drug is being used primarily to {treat} anemias.*

3. If the head is a pronoun, use the pronoun type (without coreference resolution) as the type of the argument.

4. If the head is a named entity, use the Identifinder tag as the type of the argument (BBN Identifinder, 2004).

5. If neither, use the name of the head's WordNet synset as the type of the argument.

Consider the sentence *The drug is being used primarily to {treat} anemias.* The PropBank annotation of this sentence marks *the drug* as ARG3 and *anemias* as ARG2. We turned this information into features for the classifier as shown in Figure 6.

The *verb* feature is intended to capture the bias of the verb. The *ARGX_TYPE* feature captures the type of the arguments directly. To measure the tradeoffs between various combinations of features, we randomly partitioned the data set into a training set (65% of the data), a validation set (15% of the data), and a test set (20% of the data).

6 Results

6.1 Classifier Choice

Because of its ease of use and Java compatibility, we used an updated version of the Stanford conditional log linear (aka maxent) classifier written by Dan Klein (Stanford Classifier, 2003). Maxent classifiers are designed to maximize the conditional log likelihood of the training data where the conditional likelihood of a particular class c on training example i is computed as:

$$\frac{1}{Z} exp(f_i \cdot \omega_c)$$

Here Z is a normalizing factor, f_i is the vector of features associated with example i and ω_c is the vector of weights associated with class c. Additionally, the Stanford classifier uses by default a Gaussian prior of 1 on the features, thus smoothing the feature weights and helping prevent overfitting.

6.2 Baselines

We use two different baselines to assess performance. They correspond to selecting the majority class of the training set overall or the majority class of verb specifically. The strong bias toward metaphor is reflected in the overall baseline of 93.80% for the validation set. The verb baseline is higher, 95.50% for the validation set, due to the presence of words such as *treat* which are predominantly literal.

6.3 Validation Set Results

Figure 7 shows the performance of the classifier on the feature sets described in the previous section. The overall and verb baselines are 605 and 616 out of 645 total examples in the validation set.

The first feature set we experimented with was just the verb. We then added each argument in turn; trying ARG0 (Feature Set 2), ARG1 (Feature Set 3), ARG2 (Feature Set 4) and ARG3 (Feature Set 5). Adding ARG1 gave the best performance gain.

ARG1 corresponds to the semantic role of *mover* in most of PropBank annotations for motion-related verbs. For example, *stocks* is labeled as ARG1 in both *Stocks fell 10 points* and *Stocks were being thrown out of windows*[3]. Intuitively, the mover role is highly informative in determining whether a motion verb is being used metaphorically, thus it makes sense that adding ARG1 added the single biggest

[3]This is an actual sentence from the training set.

FSet	Feature Schemas	M	L	Total	%Tot
1	*verb*	599/605	20/40	619/645	95.97
2	*verb, ARG0_TYPE*	601/605	17/40	618/645	95.81
3	*verb, ARG1_TYPE*	602/605	19/40	621/645	96.28
4	*verb, ARG2_TYPE*	600/605	19/40	619/645	95.97
5	*verb, ARG3_TYPE*	599/605	20/40	619/645	95.97
6	*verb, ARG1_TYPE, ARG3_TYPE*	602/605	19/40	621/645	96.28
7	*verb, ARG1_TYPE, ARG2_TYPE, ARG3_TYPE*	601/605	18/40	619/645	95.97
8	*verb, ARG0_TYPE, ARG1_TYPE, ARG2_TYPE*	602/605	18/40	620/645	96.12
9	*verb, ARG0_TYPE, ARG1_TYPE, ARG2_TYPE, ARG3_TYPE*	602/605	17/40	619/645	95.97

Figure 7: For each Feature Set, the feature schemas that define it, along with the ratio of correct to total examples on the validation set for metaphor (M), literal (L) and total (Total) is shown.

jump in performance compared to the other arguments.

Once we determined that ARG1 was the best argument to add, we also experimented with combining ARG1 with the other arguments. Validation results are shown for these other feature combinations (Feature Sets 6,7, 8 and 9)

Using the best feature sets (Feature Sets 3,6), 621 targets are correctly labeled by the classifier. The accuracy is 96.98%, reducing error on the validation set by 40% and 17% over the baselines.

6.4 Test Set Results

We retrained the classifier using Feature Set 3 over the training and validation sets, then tested it on the test set. The overall and verb baselines are 800 and 817 out of 861 total examples, respectively. The classifier correctly labeled 819 targets in the test set. The results, broken down by frame, are shown in Figure 8. The final accuracy of 95.12%, represents a reduction of error by 31% and 5% over the baselines.

6.5 Discussion

A comprehensive assessment of the classifier's performance requires a measure of interannotator agreement. Interannotator agreement represents a ceiling on the performance that can be expected on the classification task. Due to the very high baseline, even rare disagreements by human annotators affects the interpretation of the classifier's performance. Unfortunately, we did not have the resources available to redundantly annotate the corpus.

We examined the 42 remaining errors and categorized them into four types:

- 13 fixable errors
- 27 errors caused by verbal biases
- 2 errors caused by bias in the training set

The fixable errors are those that could be fixed given more experimentation with the feature sets and more data. Many of these errors are probably caused by the verbal bias, but a verbal bias that should not be insurmountable (for example, 2 or 3 metaphor to each 1 literal).

The 27 errors caused by verbal biases are ones where the verb is so strongly biased to a particular metaphoric class that it is unsurprising that a test example of the opposite class was missed. Verbs like *treat* (0 metaphoric to 20 literal) and *lead* (345 metaphoric to 0 literal) are in this category.

The two remaining errors are cases where the verb was not present in the training data.

7 Related Work

Previous work on automated metaphor detection includes Fass (1991), Martin (1990), and Mason (2004). Whereas our aim is to classify unseen sentences as literal or metaphorical, these projects address the related but distinct task of identifying metaphorical mappings. All three use the selectional preferences of verbs to identify metaphors. In literal usage, the arguments that fill particular roles of a verb are frequently of a common type. For instance, in the MEDICAL domain, the object of the

Frame	M	L	Total	%Tot	%OBL	%VBL
Cause_motion	78/78	1/10	79/88	**89.77**	88.64	88.64
Cotheme	179/179	0/2	179/181	98.90	98.90	98.90
Cure	26/30	3/3	29/33	87.88	**90.91**	90.91
Motion_directional	242/242	0/2	242/244	99.18	99.18	99.18
Placing	176/181	13/25	189/206	**91.75**	87.86	91.26
Self_motion	87/90	14/19	101/109	**92.66**	82.57	91.74
All_Frames	788/800	31/61	819/861	**95.12**	92.92	94.89

Figure 8: The results of the classifier on the test set, using Feature Set 6. For each frame, the ratio of correct to total examples for metaphor (M), literal (L) and total (Total) is shown. The total percent correct for the frame (%Tot), the overall baseline percentage (%OBL), and the verb baseline percentage (%VBL) are also shown. The cumulative performance over all frames is located in the bottom row of the table.

verb *treat* is usually a pathological state. In the FINANCE domain, the object of *treat* is usually an economic problem. This difference in selectional preference suggests metaphorical usage. Furthermore, it suggests a metaphorical mapping between health problems and economic problems.

The systems described by Fass and Martin exhibit impressive reasoning capabilities such as identifying novel metaphors, distinguishing metaphor from metonymy, and interpreting some metaphorical sentences. But they require hand-coded knowledge bases and thus have limited coverage and are difficult to extend. More similar to our efforts, Mason's CorMet uses a corpus-based approach. In CorMet, domains are characterized by certain keywords which are used to compile domain-specific corpora from the internet. Based on differences in selectional preferences between domains, CorMet seeks to identify metaphorical mappings between concepts in those domains.

One shortcoming of using syntactic arguments is reflected by CorMet's mistaken identification of a mapping between *institutions* and *liquids*. This arises from sentences like *The company dissolved* and *The acid dissolved the compound*. Such sentences suggest a mapping between the subjects in the target domain, *institutions*, and the subjects in source domain, *liquids*. Using semantic roles avoids this source of noise. This is not to suggest that the syntactic features are unimportant, indeed the selectional preferences determined by CorMet could be used to select which arguments to use for features in our classifier.

Our approach considers each sentence in isolation. However the distribution of metaphorical usage is not uniform in the WSJ corpus (Martin, 1994),. It is therefore possible that the information about surrounding sentences would be useful in determining whether a usage is metaphorical. CorMet incorporates context in a limited way, computing a confidence rating, based in part upon whether a metaphoric mapping co-occurs with others in a systematic way.

8 Conclusion

Metaphors are a ubiquitous phenomenon in language, and our corpus analysis clearly bears this out. It is somewhat gratifying that with a judicious combination of the available wide-coverage resources (WordNet, FrameNet, PropBank) we were able to build classifiers that could outperform the baseline even in the most skewed cases. Our results show the utility of our approach and more generally the maturity of the current NLP technology to make progress in attacking the challenging and important problem of interpreting figurative language.

However, this is only the first step. As with all semantic extraction methods and technologies, the proof of utility is not in how good the extractor is but how much it helps in an actual task. As far as we can tell, this problem remains open for the entire semantic parsing/role labeling/extraction field despite the flurry of activity in the last four years. In the case of metaphor interpretation, we have some initial encouragement from the results published by (Narayanan, 1997) and others.

Our classifier relies on PropBank senses, so we can use the high performance classifiers available for PropBank. The price is that we have to construct mappings from FrameNet frames to PropBank senses. However, this is a one-time effort pursued by many groups, so this should not present a problem to extending our approach to cover all frames and metaphors. Additionally, we are in the process of linking the metaphor detector to a metaphor inference system. We hope to have initial results to report on by conference time.

References

BBN Identifinder. 2004. http://www.bbn.com/for_government_customers/data_indexing_and_mining/identifinder.html.

Michael Collins. 1999. *Head-Driven Statistical Models of Natural Language Parsing*. Ph.D. thesis, University of Pennsylvania.

Dan Fass. 1991. Met*: a method for discriminating metonymy and metaphor by computer. *Comput. Linguist.*, 17(1):49–90.

Christine Fellbaum, editor. 1998. *WordNet: An Electronic Lexical Database*. MIT Press.

Mark Johnson. 1987. *The Body in the Mind: The Bodily Basis of Meaning, Imagination and Reason*. University of Chicago Press.

Paul Kingsbury, Martha Palmer, and Mitchell Marcus. 2002. Adding semantic annotation to the penn treebank. In *Proceedings of the Human Language Technology Conference*.

George Lakoff and Mark Johnson. 1980. *Metaphors We Live By*. University of Chicago Press.

George Lakoff and Mark Turner. 1989. *More Than Cool Reason: A Field Guide to Poetic Metaphor*. University of Chicago Press.

George Lakoff. 1994. The contemporary theory of metaphor. In Andrew Ortony, editor, *Metaphor and Thought*. Cambridge University Press.

Ronald Langacker. 1987. *Foundations of Cognitive Grammar I: Theoretical Prerequisites*. Stanford University Press.

James Martin. 1990. *Computational Model of Metaphor Interpretation*. Academic Press.

J.H. Martin. 1994. A corpus-based analysis of context effects on metaphor comprehension. Technical report, Boulder: University of Colorado: Computer Science Department.

Zachary J. Mason. 2004. Cormet: a computational, corpus-based conventional metaphor extraction system. *Comput. Linguist.*, 30(1):23–44.

Srini Narayanan and Sanda Harabagiu. 2004. Question answering based on semantic structures. In *Proceedings of the International Conference on Computational Linguistics*.

Srini Narayanan. 1997. *Knowledge-Based Action Representations for Metaphor and Aspect*. Ph.D. thesis, University of California at Berkeley.

Steve Sinha and Srini Narayanan. 2005. Model-based answer selection. In *Proceedings of the AAAI Workshop on Inference for Textual Question Answering*.

Stanford Classifier. 2003. http://nlp.stanford.edu/software/classifier.shtml.

Scaling Construction Grammar up to Production Systems: the Situated Constructional Interpretation Model

Guillaume Pitel

Langue et Dialogue
LORIA
BP239 54000 Nancy, France
Guillaume.Pitel@gmail.com

Abstract

While a great effort has concerned the development of fully integrated modular understanding systems, few researches have focused on the problem of unifying existing linguistic formalisms with cognitive processing models. The Situated Constructional Interpretation Model is one of these attempts. In this model, the notion of "construction" has been adapted in order to be able to mimic the behavior of Production Systems. The Construction Grammar approach establishes a model of the relations between linguistic forms and meaning, by the mean of constructions. The latter can be considered as pairings from a topologically structured space to an unstructured space, in some way a special kind of production rules.

1 Introduction

Accounting for pragmatical and cognitive phenomena in a linguistic formalism is a challenging task whose resolution would be of great benefit for many fields of linguistics, especially those dealing with interpretation in a context. In domains such as practical dialogue or embodied understanding, there would be a real gain in dealing with environment data the same way one deals with linguistic data. These kinds of systems currently need *ad hoc* heuristics or representations. These heuristics are implemented in modules that are often impossible to reuse for another task than the one they were developed for. This point particularly concerns phenomena that lay at the interface of linguistics and general cognition, such as vagueness (Ballweg, 1983), reference resolution (Brown-Schmidt, 2003; Reboul, 1999), or modeling of cognitive representations (Langacker, 1983; Talmy, 1988).

Similarly, accounting for linguistic phenomena in a psychologically motivated model is far from simple. The attempts in that direction are often limited to simple phenomena, because all linguistic formalisms rely on principles slightly or totally different from those of cognitive architectures.

The definitive solution to this problem is probably still far from reach, but nevertheless, I think that the maturity of cognitive linguistics and the consequent emergence of language analyzers connected to cognitive architectures is an excellent direction toward a unified theory mixing linguistic and psychological models. The Embodied Construction Grammar or ECG (Bergen, 2003) and its analyzer (Bryant, 2003) are a good example of such an effort, even though it does not go beyond the linguistic layer since mental simulation is left to a mental simulation module based on the notion of x-schema (Narayanan, 2001).

Consequently, I try to propose a model that conciliates a linguistic theory with a cognitive architecture. The choice of the linguistic theory naturally goes to Construction Grammar (Fillmore, 1988; Kay 2002) and Frame Semantics (Fillmore, 1982), due to the parallel one can draw between a production rule and a construction, and the cogni-

Proceedings of the 3rd Workshop on Scalable Natural Language Understanding, pages 49–56,
New York City, June 2006.

tive architecture is, obviously, the family of Production Systems (Newell, 1990; Anderson, 1993). Moreover, since many pragmatical models rely on topologically structured representation, I introduce the notion of **context**, a notion that has never been adapted to these theories in order to organize data in "storages" structured in dissimilar ways.

1.1 Typical Problem

Consider a situation where a user can command a software to manipulate some very simple objects (colored geometrical objects of various sizes). The user may say (a) "Put the small red square on the left", (b) "Remove the small red square on the left" or (c) "Move the small red square on the left".

First, these three utterances may involve different parsing depending on the actual environment of the utterance, at least for those with "put" and "move". Second, the "square" targeted by the user may be a rectangle in the actual software representation, with slightly different width and height. It may also be relatively small compared to other red squares, but bigger than other objects, and relatively red compared to other non-square objects.

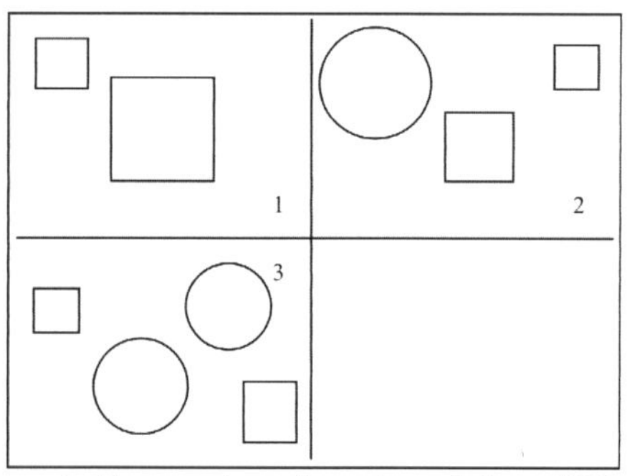

Figure 1: Some situations involving different understandings (without color).

Imagine what happens in the different situations illustrated in Figure 1. In situation 1, for instance, (a) would not be understandable, since the small square is already on the left, while (c) could lead to the one argument sense of "move", i.e. "move *something* somewhere else", not to the two arguments version "move *something somewhere*" (actually, the one-argument sense is an implicit understanding of the destination allowed by "move", so the difference should not be lexicalized). In situation 2, (b) and (c) would lead to two different interpretations of the referring expression "the small red square on the left": in (b), it refers to the square in the center (with a possible wavering), while it preferably refers to the square on the right in (c). In situation 3, (c) may be interpreted with the one argument sense of "move", and will target the square on the left since it is the smallest, but there should be a strong hesitation, since the other square is not that bigger, and the two arguments sense of "move" is intuitively preferred. At the same time (a) will target the square on the right, which is relatively small compared to the neighboring circles, but would raise incomprehension if the circles were missing.

In general, in order to take those facts into account, it is necessary either to produce all possible analyzes at each layer of the interpretation (which is quite problematic if it is desirable to allow for imperfect analyzes), or to allow two-ways interactions between the layers of interpretation (for instance, the pragmatic layer talking back to the semantic layer about the fact that the original position of an object is the same as the requested destination, which may indicate a wrong analysis).

My proposal is to allow for a generic capacity of interaction between the states of the interpretation (speaking about states is better than about layers since the latter presupposes something about the organizing of the interpretation), based on a unified operation between all the possible states. More specifically, the idea is to merge the notions from construction grammar and productions systems.

1.2 Merging Construction Grammar and Production Systems

Merging a linguistic analyzer with a cognitive processing model may seem a bit useless since they do not share the same objective. Linguistic analyzer's goal is to provide a formal model for the representation of linguistic knowledge, accordingly to linguistic observations. Cognitive models, on the other hand, aim at helping the modeling of real cognitive processing, in order to compare theoretical model of perception processing with real data from experiments. Cognitive models like production systems being Turing-equivalent, they typically do not lack of any expressiveness, meaning that anything one can describe with any linguistic representation could be implemented within a cognitive model (hopefully, since linguistic competence is part of the cognitive competence).

However, to my knowledge, no attempt to try describing a linguistic competence within a cognitive model has gone a long way. Existing researches on that topic have focused on very narrow problems, and what is more important, have been tightened to very small lexicons (Emond, 1997; Ball, 2003; Fowles-Winkler and Michaelis, 2005).

My analysis of this problem is that production systems are too permissive to allow a human to describe a grammar with a reasonable effort. More specifically, all generalization links that exist between grammar rules should be encoded in some explicit way in a production system.

Furthermore, linguistic formalisms are designed in such way to only express all possible human languages. In other words, a linguistic formalism is successful when it is flexible enough to describe all linguistic phenomena, while being human-readable enough to allow for a large-scale grammar development. As a consequence, linguistic formalisms are too restrictive to allow dealing with cognitive processes like the ones described using production systems.

Putting together a linguistic formalism and a model of pragmatical and cognitive processing implies to make a choice among all the current theories. Given the large predominance of production systems in cognitive modeling, it seems quit-

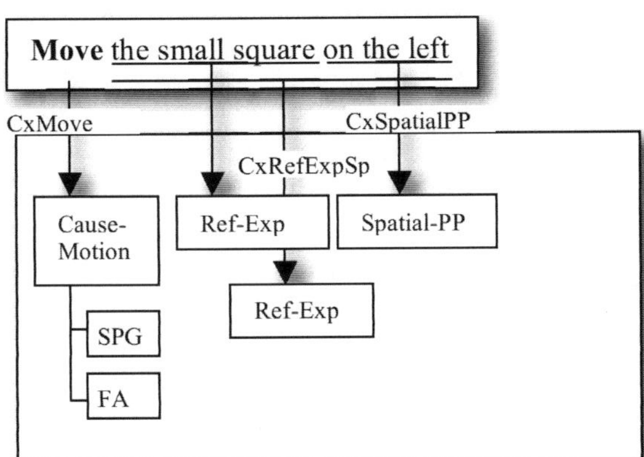

Figure 3: First step of analysis, the global construction (Imperative) is not active yet.

natural to choose them as the cognitive model. The choice for the linguistic formalism is more open. Previous attempts of linguistic modeling in cognitive models have used $\overline{X}$ theory, categorical grammar or construction grammar. My pick has been the construction grammar because it shares some interesting features with production systems, and and because it deals directly with semantic, contrary to other grammatical theories. Particularly, constructions are pairing between too poles: form and meaning, this is very similar to the notion of a production taking one input from a chunk, and producing its output into another one.

1.3 Example of processing

In such an approach, what should happen when interpreting "*move the small square on the left*" in situation 3 on the Figure 1? The first step of the analysis (simplified for sake of clarity), illustrated in Figure 3, shows how "move" produces a predicate that encompasses a *Cause-Motion* schema, itself evoking a *Source-Path-Goal* (SPG) and a *Force-Action* (FA) schema. The *CxMove* construction adds a constraint about the fact that *source* and *goal* should differ.

After this, two constructions *CxImperative* can connect, through their *theme* role, the referents evoked by the *RefExp* shemas (each construction being one possible interpretation) with the *source* of the *Source-Path-Goal*. The *CxImperative* encapsulates the predicate in a *Request* schema. Another construction can connect the *goal* of the *Source-Path-Goal* with the *Spatial-PP* produced from "on the left", with the predicate modified by the construction that took its *RefExp* from "the small square".

At this point, the "mental simulation" required

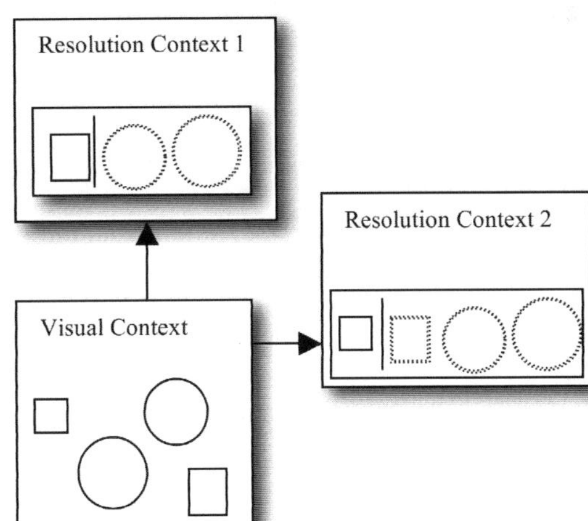

Figure 2: Mental simulation of the reference resolution

to resolve the referents can start. This step is illustrated in a very simplified way in Figure 2. The complete process is described in (Pitel, 2004; Pitel

& Sansonnet, 2003) and processes potential referents through several sorting steps, one for each referential predicate (here: *square* and *small* in Resolution Context 1 from the two-arguments move interpretation; *square, small* and *on the left* in Resolution Context 2 from the other one). The process is described with the kind of constructions defined by the SCIM.

2 Basic Notions of the SCIM

The Situated Constructional Interpretation model (SCIM) describes how information can be processed in a way that is both linguistically and psychologically plausible. It relies on three notions: **schemas** are for low-level data description, **contexts** are for describing the organization of instances of schemas, and **s-constructions** represent the mean to process data. Eventually, a SCIM-based interpretation system will run instances of s-constructions that take and produce instances of schemas situated in instances of contexts. These three notions are partly inherited from the ECG.

2.1 Schemas

Schemas are *constrained, typed features structures,* with an *inheritance* mechanism and no type disjunction. Schemas are a kind of data type. They describe complex structures of information used to represent the state of the running interpretation. As shown in Figure 4, schemas are defined with three blocks:

- **inherits** *schema-name$_1$*, ... which specifies from which schema(s) this one inherits from. a specific case of the schema *x*, it inherits all of its properties (roles and constraints).
- **roles**, which specifies a list of roles, constrained to a given schema type or atomic type (Integer, Boolean, String, or user-defined enumerations of symbols).
- **constraints**, which specify the constraints that must be verified in order for an instance of the schema to be a valid one. A constraint can be a *predicate* if the role has an atomic type, or an *identification* constraint (asserting that two roles must share the same value), or a *filler* constraint with a constant value.

An **instance of schema** is moreover described by values attached to its roles (some or all of them may be left underspecified), a unique identifier, a positive value representing its informative capacity, a percentage of trust level, and the list of its parents' identifiers. A parent of an instance of schema is an instance of schema "used" in the process that led to its production. It is thus possible, in a s-construction, to know whether two given instances of schema are somehow related to each other in the interpretation process.

```
schema <schema-id>
inherits <schema-id_0, ..., schema-id_n>
Roles
[?]<local-type-id>:<atomic-type-id>
[?]<local-context-id>:<context-id>[@<local-context-id>]
[?]<local-schema-id>:<schema-id>[@<local-context-id>]
Constraints
<boolean-operation>(<constraint_0>, ..., <constraint_n>)
<role-id> ← <atomic-value>|<function>(<atomic-
value>,...)
<role-id> ↔ <role-id>|<C-function>(<role-id>)
<role-id> = <role-id>
<boolean-predicate>(<role-id_0>, ..., <role-id_n>)
```

```
a <role-id> is one of:
  self (optional if not used alone)
  <local-type-id>
  <local-context-id>
  <local-schema-id>
  <inherited-schema>*<inherited-role-id>
  <role-id>.<sub-role-id>
```

Figure 4: Schema definition formalism.

From the production systems perspective, schemas define the type of features that can be attached to a category. Basically, in that point of view, an instance of schema is a *chunk* and roles are *slots*.

Schemas hierarchy

Schemas can inherit roles and constraints from other schemas. That means that schemas are organized in a multiple inheritance hierarchy. In order to avoid ambiguity in role access, inherited roles must be accessed through an inheritance path. For instance, accessing the role *color* in a schema *Square*, if the hierarchy is Figure→Rectangle→Square, and where the color role is declared in the Figure schema, would be realized through this kind of path: Rectangle*Figure*color.

Inheritance also means that an instance of schema S can be unified with a role whose type is R if S == R **or** if R is one of the parents of S.

One problem with this approach of inheritance is that, in order to fulfill the Liskov substitution principle (Liskov, 1988), it is sometimes necessary to use unnatural type hierarchies (stating that Square doesn't inherit from Rectangle, for instance). I am very mindful about this problem, since such a discrepancy is quite tedious for a model that aims to approximate the human way of processing information, but this problem is out of the scope of this paper[1].

Constraints

A schema declaration contains a set of constraints that must be satisfied in order for an instance of this schema to be considered valid. Constraints are specified with six basic forms:

- Type constraints on roles.
- Boolean operation (OR, NOT, NAND,...) connecting several constraints.
- **Filler** constraint symbolized by a single arrow (←) specifies that a constant, atomic value must fill the role in an instance.
- **Identification** constraint, symbolized by a double-headed arrow (↔), specifies that both sides of the constraint must unify, that is, all roles' values must be compatible with each other.
- An equality constraint (=) that constrains two roles to refer to the same instance.
- A **boolean predicate** constraint can be asserted between any number of roles.

Another kind of constraint, on the places occupied by instances of schema in context, will be explained in the section about s-constructions, as will the role of interrogation marks in the schema declaration formalism.

2.2 Contexts

A *context* declaration is a description of a container that can hold instances of schemas. In other words, it describes a space (including the topology part that can be specified by a set of relations and operations) that can contain pointers to instances of schemas at given *places*.

The notion of context inherits all of the properties of the notion of schema. Actually, a context is really a kind of schema and, as a consequence, a schema's role can be restricted to be a context. A declaration of context adds three more blocks to the declaration of a schema, as shown in Figure 5:

- **places** declare a list of *opaque* types (the internal structure of the type is hidden in the implementation) that describe an acceptable position in the context. Instances of schema (or context) that will be contained in an instance of this context will be linked with a position whose type is one (and only one) of the declared *places*. Examples of places are: *point, segment, multi-segment, line, box, disc, ...*

context *<context-id>*
inherits *<context-id*$_0$, ..., context-*id*$_n$>
Roles
// idem schemas roles
Constraints
// idem schemas constraints
Places
<place-id>
Relations
<relation-id(<place-id>, <place-id>,...)> ↦ *<type-id>*
// for instance: before(point, point) ↦ Boolean
Operations
<operation-id>(*<place-id>*, *<place-id>*,...) ↦ *<place-id>*
// for instance: intersection(segment, segment) ↦ segment

Figure 5: Context definition formalism

- **relations** are functions that associate a value in an atomic domain from one or more *places*. Relations define constraints on the positions of a set of instances of schema. For instance, one can define a precedence relation in a linear context.

[1] We consider that this problem could be solved by the approach called "Points of View Theory" (which is not related to inter-person points of view), proposed by Pitel (2004). In this theory, there is no type hierarchy, and the ability to substitute a representation by another is described by rules that can take the dynamic context into account. In this approach, types do not represent concepts, but points of view on perceptions (in the wide meaning), and transition from one point of view to the other is context-dependent.

- **operations** are functions that associate a *position* from one or more *positions*. For instance, a union of segments is an operation.

Terminologically, an instance of schema (or context) located in a context, that is, an instance with a place, will be called a **situated instance**, whereas an instance of schema (or context) simply connected to another instance by a role will just be called a **role instance**.

The only explicit equivalent to contexts in ECG is the notion of **space**, which describes Fauconnier's mental spaces (Fauconnier, 1985). Implicit contexts are however used in Construction Grammar: the **form pole**, which stores instances of schemas representing linguistic data in a linear space, and the unstructured **meaning pole**.

```
s-construction <s-construction-id>
inherits <s-construction-id0, ..., s-construction-idn>
roles // idem schema's roles
constructional
  <local-s-constr-id>: <s-construction-id>
constituents
  <local-ctx-id>: <context-id>[@<local-ctx-id>]/I|O|IO
  <local-constit-id>: <schema-id>[@<local-ctx-id>]/I|O|IO
constraints
  // idem schemas constraints, plus :
  // a role-id can be marked as muted: ?<role-id>
  // a place-id is either a <local-constit-id> or the result of a
context operation like:
  // <local-ctx-id>.<context-operation-id>(<place-id>, ...)
  <role-id> ⊂ <role-id> // right hand side must be parent
  <local-ctx-id>.<context-relation-id>(<place-id>, ...)
  OUT(<local-constit-id>) // remove the situated instance
```

Figure 6: S-construction definition formalism

2.3 S-constructions

S-constructions are situated constructions, that is, constructions that describe the relations between several instances of schemas located in structured contexts. As for the notion of context, the notion of s-construction is derived from the schemas, because the s-construction itself can hold information. Besides that, the declaration of a s-construction contains:

- A **constructional** block that describes the other instances of s-constructions this s-construction relies on. The block contains a list of label: s-construction-name declarations. Any restriction on the constituents of those instances of s-construction is described as a constraint on label.constituent in the **constraints** block.
- A **constituents** block that describes the instances of contexts and schemas constrained by the s-construction (note that the meaning of constituents is different than in ECG). The declaration of those constituents specifies whether the instance must preexist and/or whether it may be created or specified by the s-construction's constraints. From a production system point of view, it means that we describe which instances are in the input, and which one are produced.

S-constructions hierarchy

Like schemas, s-constructions are organized in a multiple inheritance hierarchy. Moreover, s-constructions benefit from a mechanism of *constructional dependence*, held by the constructional block. Those two notions are, to some extent, redundant. Indeed, inheriting from a s-construction is equivalent to having an instance of this s-construction in the constructional block. However, one can have two different instances of the same s-construction in the constructional block, whereas it is impossible to inherit twice from the same s-construction. Moreover, it is possible to add a negative semantics in the constructional block, in order to assert that some instance of s-construction must not have occurred to satisfy the s-construction's conditions.

The *constructional* block is thus more powerful than the classical inheritance relation, but as for the schemas hierarchy, it is not within the scope of this paper to discuss about the inheritance relations between s-constructions. A declaration of s-construction is thus, from that point of view, in conformance with the standard view shared in construction grammars.

Situated aspects of s-constructions

A s-construction can "choose" instances of schemas, given positional constraints in the context where the instances of schemas are stored. Then, the s-construction will "create" new instances of context or schemas, or will specify some previously underspecified role's value. S-constructions can connect together more than two instances of schema. To that extent, it differs from ECG's construction (ECG's way of doing so makes use of an evoke block).

The specification of structural constraints is very similar to the other constraints. A structural constraint looks like this: context-id.relation(roles-in-context-id). Basically, a context relation is considered as a boolean predicate constraint. The main difference is that, instead of specifying the roles, such a constraint specifies the place of the instance of schema referred to by the role.

Dynamic aspects

The biggest gap between productions systems and construction grammar is the difference between the dynamic nature of productions versus the declarative nature of linguistic constructions. For instance, a typical rule in a production system (from the ACT-R tutorial) would be represented in Figure 7. In order to take this possibility into account, it is necessary to introduce at some point some imperative features in the s-construction.

Imperative features are introduced through several mechanisms. The first one is about role instances, the second one is about situated instances and the third one is about specifying constituents acting as inputs and/or outputs.

ACT-R declaration	**English description**
(p start	
=goal>	If the goal is
ISA count-from	to count from
start =num1	the number =num1
step start	and the step is start
==>	Then
=goal>	*change* the goal
step counting	to note that one is now counting
+retrieval>	and request a retrieval
ISA count-order	of a count-order fact
first =num1	for the number that follows =num1
)	

Figure 7: Example of ACT-R rule with a value changing

- **Mutable roles**. In the **roles** blocks, they are specified by a question mark (?). If a role is marked as mutable in a schema declaration, then it can be accessed through two means in a s-construction constraint. The usual way constrains the state of the role instance *before* the application of the s-construction, the mutated way constrains the state of the role instance *after* the application of the s-construction.
- **Removable situated instances**. The constraint *OUT(<constituent-id>)* specifies that the situated instance must be marked as not being present anymore in its context, after execution of the s-construction.
- **Input and/or output constituents**. Each constituent of a s-construction is marked with a symbol /I or /O, stating whether the situated instance should be present before and whether it will be modified.

3 Computational Aspects

Given the characteristics of the SCIM, its expressiveness and its procedural orientation, one cannot occult the problems that it raises from the computational point of view. Building an implementation of the Situated Constructional Interpretation Model definitely means to give up the idea of conducting a complete exploration of the search space.

The main problem is that two s-constructions may lead to contradictory constraints. In other words, one must keep track of all the decisions and explore all the possibilities.

The problem is even worse with mutable instances, since some constraints may be satisfied at some moment in one possible interpretation, while being unsatisfied at another moment. This time dependence must be handled very carefully, and adds some complexity to the processing of constraints.

However, the model also presents some interesting features, computationally speaking. For instance, it is quite easy to add a weighting layer to the SCIM, in order to simulate expectation, informational potential, or execution cost. Such a layer could be trained to learn how to lead to the best interpretations at a minimal cost.

4 Conclusion

In this paper I propose and describe a model of interpretation both linguistically and psychologically motivated. This model allows describing a construction grammar as well as a production system, with three basic notions: *schemas*, *contexts* and *s-constructions*. Applications for such a model are wide, from more integrated dialogue systems to a unified theory of cognition and language.

A longer description of the processing architecture would be necessary in order to really confront the hypotheses I made in the section "Computational aspects", but nevertheless, one can already draw a parallel between this model with a spatial structuring of information, and the structure that neuromimetic models can handle. Also, incomplete exploration of the search space, guided by a cost/gain approach, has previously been proposed as a plausible model of processing for human cognition. More than computational efficiency, the goal of this model is to propose a formalism that would be easier to use both for linguistic and cognitive modeling, in order to observe and act on the simulated processing of language and other cognitive functions.

Many of the claims in this paper have yet to be proved through the implementation of the SCIM, and cognitive modeling using the system. Since many processing models have been made both on construction grammar and production systems, important researches should be easy enough to reuse in the SCIM.

References

John R. Anderson (1993). *Rules of the Mind.* Erlbaum, Hillsdale, NJ.

Jerry T. Ball (2003). Beginnings of a language comprehension module in ACT-R 5.0. In F. Detje, D. Doerner, & H. Schaub (Eds.), In *Proceedings of the Fifth International Conference on Cognitive Modeling* (pp. 231-232). Bamberg, Germany: Universitats-Verlag Bamberg.

Joachim Ballweg (1983). Vagueness or context-dependence? supervaluation revisited in a semantics based on scales. In T. T. Ballmer and M. Pinkal, editors, *Approaching Vagueness*, pages 59--78. North Holland, Amsterdam.

Benjamin K. Bergen & Nancy Chang (2003). Embodied construction grammar in simulation-based language understanding. In J.-O. Ostman and M. Fried, editors, *Construction Grammar(s): Cognitive and Cross-Language Dimensions*. John Benjamins,

Sarah Brown-Schmidt & Michael K. Tanenhaus (2003). Referential domains and the interpretation of referring expressions in interactive conversation. In *Proc. of Diabruck 2003, Seventh Workshop on the Semantics and Pragmatics of Dialogue (SEMDIAL).*

Johno Bryant (2003). *Constructional analysis*. Master's thesis, University of California at Berkeley,

Bruno Emond (1997). Modeling natural language comprehension and anaphora resolution with ACT-R. In *Proceedings of the Fourth Annual ACT-R Workshop* (pp. 1-8). Pittsburgh, PA: Department of Psychology, Carnegie Mellon University.

Fauconnier, G. (1985). *Mental Spaces: Aspects of Meaning Construction in Natural Language.* MIT Press/Bradford, Cambridge, Mass. and London.

Fillmore, C. J. (1982). Frame Semantics. In L. S. of Korea, editor, *Linguistic in the Morning Calm*, pages 111--38. Hanshin, Seoul.

Fillmore, C. J. (1988). The Mechanisms of Construction Grammar. *Berkeley Linguistics Society*, 14:0 35—55.

Anna M. Fowles-Winkler & Laura Michaelis (2005) An ACT-R model of sentence sorting with argument structure constuctions. In the *Proceedings of the Linguistic Society of America Annual Meeting*, January 7, 2005, Oakland, CA.

Kay, P. (2002). An informal sketch of a formal architecture for construction grammar. *Grammars*, 5:0 1—19.

Langacker, R. W. (1987). *Foundations of Cognitive Grammar*, volume 1. Stanford University Press.

Liskov, B. (1988). Data abstraction and hierarchy. *SIGPLAN Notices*, 230 (5), 1988.

Newell, A. (1990). *Unified Theories of Cognition.* Harvard University Press, Cambridge, MA.

Pitel, G. and Sansonnet, J.-P. (2003) Unified Representation of Typological, Absolute and Relational Predicates. In *Proceedings of PACLING'03*. Avail. on first author web page.

Pitel, G. (2004). MICO: la notion de construction située pour un modèle d'interprétation et de résolution de la réference pour le dialogue finalisé. PhD Thesis, Université Paris XI.

Reboul, A. (1999). Reference, agreement, evolving reference and the theory of mental representation. In M. Coene, W. D. Mulder, P. Dendale, and Y. D'Hulst, Eds. *Studia Linguisticae in honorem Lilianae Tasmowski*, pages 601—616. Unipress, Padova.

Talmy, L. (1988). Force dynamics in language and cognition. *Cognitive Science*, 12:0 49—100.

Searching for Grammar Right

Vanessa Micelli
European Media Laboratory
Schloss-Wolfsbrunnenweg 33
69118 Heidelberg, Germany
{firstname.lastname@eml-d.villa-bosch.de}

Abstract

This paper describes our ongoing work in and thoughts on developing a grammar learning system based on a construction grammar formalism. Necessary modules are presented and first results and challenges in formalizing the grammar are shown up. Furthermore, we point out the major reasons why we chose construction grammar as the most fitting formalism for our purposes. Then our approach and ideas of learning new linguistic phenomena, ranging from holophrastic constructions to compositional ones, is presented.

1 Introduction

Since any particular language[1] changes constantly (Cf. Hopper and Traugott, 2003; Bybee, 1998) – and even varies across domains, users, registers etc. – scalable natural language understanding systems must be able to cope with language variation and change. Moreover, due to the fact that any natural language understanding system, which is based on some formal representation of that language's grammar, will always only be able to represent a portion of what is going on in any particular language at the present time, we need to find systematic ways of endowing natural language understanding systems with means of learning new forms, new meanings and, ultimately, new form-meaning pairings, i.e. constructions.

Constructions are the basic building blocks, posited by a particular grammar framework called Construction Grammar, and are defined as follows: "C is a construction iff_{def} C is a form-meaning pair $\langle F_i, S_i \rangle$ such that some aspect of F_i or some aspect of S_i is not strictly predictable from C's component parts or from other previously established constructions." (Goldberg, 1995:4).

Construction Grammar originated from earlier insights in functional and usage-based models of language mainly supposed by cognitive linguists (e.g. Lakoff, 1987; Fillmore and Kay, 1987; Kay, 2002; Talmy, 1988; etc.). It has been devised to handle actually occurring natural language, which notoriously contains non-literal, elliptic, context-dependent, metaphorical or underspecified linguistic expressions. These phenomena still present a challenge for today's natural language understanding systems. In addition to these advantages, we adhere to principles proposed by other constructivists as e.g. Tomasello (2003) that language acquisition is a usage-based phenomenon, contrasting approaches by generative grammarians who assume an innate grammar (Chomsky, 1981). Furthermore, we agree to the idea that grammatical phenomena also contribute to the semantics of a sentence which is the reason why syntax cannot be defined independently of semantics of a grammar. A more detailed outline of construction grammar and the principles we adhered to in formalizing it will be given in sections 2 and 3.

The input to the system is natural language data as found on the web, as e.g. in news tickers or blogs, initially restricted to the soccer domain. As

[1] This claim also holds within any solidified system of conventionalized form-meaning pairings, e.g. dialects, chronolects, sociolects, idiolects, jargons, etc.

Proceedings of the 3rd Workshop on Scalable Natural Language Understanding, pages 57–64,
New York City, June 2006. ©2006 Association for Computational Linguistics

the learning process develops the input will gradually be extended to other domains. A description of the corpus and its selection process will be given in section 4. Section 5 provides an outlook on the learning paradigm, while the last section presents some future issues and conclusions.

2 Grammar Formalism

The most crucial foundation that is needed to build a grammar learning system is a grammar formalism. Therefore, we are designing a new formalization of construction grammar called ECtoloG (Porzel et al., 2006; Micelli et al., in press).

One existing formal computational model of construction grammar is the Embodied Construction Grammar (ECG) (Chang et al., 2002; Bergen and Chang, 2002), with its main focus being on language understanding and later simulation[2]. A congruent and parallel development has led to FCG which simulates the emergence of language (Steels, 2005). FCG is mainly based on the same primitives and operators as ECG is. We decided to employ ECG in our model mainly for historical reasons (see details about its development in the following section), adhering to its main primitives and operators, but employing the state of the art in knowledge representation. We adopt insights and mechanisms of FCG where applicable.

2.1 Construction Grammar and ECG

One main difference between West Coast Grammar (Langacker, 1987; Lakoff, 1987) and East Coast Grammar (Chomsky, 1965; Katz, 1972) is the fact that construction grammar offers a vertical – not a horizontal – organisation of any knowledge concerning a language's grammar. That is, that generative grammars split form from function. Syntax, morphology, a lexicon or other formal components of the grammar constitute form, while the conventional function is defined by semantics.

All constructions of a language, however, form in Langacker's terms "a structured inventory of conventional linguistic units" (Langacker, 1987:54). This inventory is network-structured, i.e. there are at least taxonomic links among the constructions (Diessel, 2004). This structure presents one of the main differences between generative and construction grammars (Croft, to appear). One of the most cited examples that evidences the necessity, that there can be no explicit separation between syntax and semantics, is Goldberg's example sentence (Goldberg, 1995:29):

(1) *he sneezed the napkin off the table.*

The whole meaning of this sentence cannot be gathered from the meanings of the discrete words. The direct object *the napkin* is not postulated by the verb *to sneeze*. This intransitive verb would have three arguments in a lexico-semantic theory: 'X causes Y to move Z by sneezing'. Goldberg states that the additional meaning of caused motion which is added to the conventional meaning of the verb *sneeze* is offered by the respective caused-motion construction. Based on this background ECG – a formal computational model of construction grammar – was developed within the Neural Theory of Language project (NTL) and the EDU project (EDU).

While other approaches consider language as completely independent from the organism which uses it, ECG claims that several characteristics of the user's sensorimotor system can influence his or her language (Gallese and Lakoff, 2005). The needed dynamic and inferential semantics in ECG is represented by embodied schemas. These schemas are known under the term of *image schemas* in traditional cognitive semantics and constitute schematic recurring patterns of sensorimotor experience (Johnson, 1987; Lakoff, 1987).

The current ASCII format of ECG is insufficient for building scalable NLU systems in the long run. Therefore, our attempt at formalizing construction grammar results in an ontological model that combines two ontological modeling frameworks endowed with a construction grammar layer, based on the main ideas behind ECG. The following section describes the resulting ontology, pointing out main challenges and advantages of that approach.

3 Formalizing Construction Grammar

The ontological frameworks mentioned above are *Descriptions & Situations* (D&S) (Gangemi and Mika, 2003) and *Ontology of Information Objects* (OIO) (Guarino, 2006), which both are extensions of the *Descriptive Ontology for Linguistic and*

[2] For a detailed ECG analysis of a declarative utterance, i.e. the sentence *Harry walked into the cafe*, see Bergen and Chang (2002).

Cognitive Engineering (DOLCE) (Masolo et al., 2003).

D&S is an ontology for representing a variety of reified contexts and states of affairs. In contrast to physical objects or events, the extensions of ontologies to the domain of non-physical objects pose a challenge to the ontology engineer. The reason for this lies in the fact that non-physical objects are taken to have meaning only in combination with some other *ground* entity. Accordingly, their logical representation is generally set at the level of theories or models and not at the level of concepts or relations (see Gangemi and Mika, 2003). It is, therefore, important to keep in mind that the meaning of a given linguistic expression emerges only through the combination of both linguistic and conceptual knowledge with "basic" ontological knowledge, as modeled in such ground ontologies.

Next to the support via dedicated editors and inference engines, one of the central advantages of our ensuing ontological model over the currently used ASCII-format of ECG lies in its compatibility with other ground ontologies developed within the Semantic Web framework.[3]

3.1 Modeling of Constructions

Constructions are modeled in the ECtoloG as information-objects. According to the specification of the OIO, information objects have – amongst others – the following properties: They are social objects realizable by some entity and they can express a description, which represents in this ontology the ontological equivalent of a meaning or a conceptualization. Since a construction constitutes a pairing of form and meaning according to the original theory of construction grammar, both properties are of advantage for our ontological model. To keep the construction's original structure, the form pole can be modeled with the help of the *realized-by* property[4] while the meaning pole is built via the *edns:expresses* property. Both processes are described more detailed in the following section.

Holophrastic Constructions

The class of lexical constructions is modeled as a subclass of *referringConstruction*. Since it is a subclass of the class *information-object* it inherits the *edns:expresses* property. The *referringConstruction* class has a restriction on this property that denotes, that at least one of the values of the *edns:expresses* property is of type *schema*. Modeling this restriction is done by means of the built-in *owl:someValuesFrom* constraint. The restriction counts for all constructions that *express* a *schema*. It has no effect on the whole class of *constructions*, i.e. it is possible that there exist constructions that do not *express* a single schema, as e.g. compositional ones, whose meaning is a composite of all constructions and schemas that constitute that compositional construction.

The form pole of each construction is modeled with the help of the *realized-by* property. This property designates that a (physical) representation – as e.g. the orthographic form of the construction – realizes a non-physical object – in this case our construction. This property is also inherited from the class *information-object,* the superclass of constructions. What fills the range of that property is the class of *edns:physical-realization*. Therefore, we define an instance of *inf:writing,* which then fills the form pole of the respective construction. This instance has once more a relation which connects it to instances of the class *inf:word* which designate the realization of the instance of the *inf:writing* class.

This way of modeling the form pole of each lexical construction enables us to automatically populate our model with new instances of constructions, as will be described more detailed in section 5.1.

Analogous to the modeling of meaning in the original ECG, the meaning pole is 'filled' with an instance of the class of *image schema*. This can be done with the help of the *edns:expresses* relation. This relation is defined, according to the specification of the D&S ontology, as a relation between information objects that are used as representations (signs) and their content, i.e. their meaning or conceptualization. In this ontology, content is reified as a description, which offered us the possibility to model image schemas as such. How image schemas are modeled will be described in section 3.2.

Compositional Constructions

Compositional constructions are constructions which are on a higher level of abstraction than holophrastic ones. This means, that there exist constructions which combine different constructions

[3] For more details see Porzel et al. (2006).

[4] We adhere to the convention to present both ontological properties, classes, and instances in italics.

into one unit. ECG designed a so-called constructional block, wherein several constructions are subsumed under and accessible in one more complex construction.

An example is the DetNoun construction, which combines a determiner and a noun to form one unit. There is the possibility to model different constraints both in the form pole and in the meaning pole of a construction. A form constraint applying to this exact construction is determining that the determiner comes before the noun. This understanding of *before* corresponds to Allen's definition of his interval relations (Allen, 1983), which states that they don't necessarily have to follow each other but that there could be some modifiers in between the two components of this construction.

A meaning constraint of this construction determines, that the meaning of the noun, used in this respective construction, is assigned to the meaning of the resulting complex construction.[5] To be able to represent these phenomena, we firstly defined a class *construction-parameter*, that denotes a subclass of *edns:parameter*, a subclass of *edns:concept*. There is a property restriction on the class that states that all values of the *requisite-for* property have to be of type *construction*. This determines instances of the class *construction-parameter* to be used only in constructions on a higher level of abstraction. All constructions used on level 0 of a grammar[6], i.e. lexical constructions, are at the same time instances of the class *construction-parameter* so that they can be used in more abstract constructions. The form and meaning constraints still need to be modeled in our framework. To determine which constructions are used in which more abstract construction, new properties are defined. These properties are subproperties of the *requisite-for* property. An example is the *requisite-detnoun-akk-sg* property. This property defines that the accusative singular determiner construction and the corresponding noun construction can be *requisite-for* the compositional construction that combines these two lexical constructions into one noun phrase.

[5] For further information about which operators are used to model these features in ECG we refer to Bergen and Chang (2002), Chang et al. (2002) and Bryant (2004).

[6] Following Bryant's (2004) division of constructions into 5 levels of different degrees of schematicity.

3.2 Modeling of Image Schemas

Following Johnson and Lakoff (Johnson, 1987; Lakoff and Johnson, 1980; Lakoff, 1987) image schemas are schematic representations that capture recurrent patterns of sensorimotor experience. According to ECG, a schema is a description whose purpose is filling the meaning pole of a construction. It consists of a list of schematic roles that can serve as simulation parameters.

In ECG, schemas can be evoked by or can evoke other schemas, i.e. particular schematic-roles of another schema can be imported. A schema can, therefore, be defined against the background of another schema[7]. The property *evokes* and its inverse property *evoked-by* have been defined as subproperties of the *dol:generically-dependent-on* property and its inverse property *dol:generic-dependent* respectively. Generic dependence is defined in the DOLCE ontology as the dependence on an individual of a given type at some time.

The class of *image schemas* is modeled as a subclass of *edns:description* (see definition of description in 3.1), in order to enable being employed in the meaning pole of constructions.

Schematic Roles

The class of *schematic-roles* is a subclass of the *edns:concept* class. In the specification of D&S a concept is classified as a non-physical object which again is defined by a description. Its function is classifying entities from a ground ontology in order to build situations that can satisfy the description. Schematic roles are parameters that allow other schemas or constructions to refer to the schema's key variable features, e.g. the role of a trajector in a Trajector Landmark-Schema can be played by the same entity that denotes the mover in e.g. a caused-motion schema.

At the moment, they are modeled with the help of the *edns:defines* property. A schema defines its schematic roles with this property, denoting a subproperty of the *edns:component* property. According to the D&S specification, a component is a proper part with a role or function in a system or a context. It is also stated, that roles can be different for the same entity, and the evaluation of them changes according to the kind of entity. This means, that instances of the class *schema* and its

[7] To clarify this claim see Langacker's hypotenuse example (Langacker, 1987:183ff.).

subclasses can have instances of the class *schematic-role* as their components. The *schematic-roles* class has to fulfil the necessary condition, that at least one of the values of the *edns:defined-by* property is of type *schema*.

The domain of the *defines* property is a *description* (which can be our schemas) and its range is set to either *concepts* or *figures* (which are our schematic roles). The problem occurring hereby is that the roles cannot be filled by complete classes which is necessary in a lot of cases, since the parameters are not always filled with atomic values but possibly with whole classes of entities. Therefore, one could think about modeling schematic roles as properties, setting the domain on the corresponding *schema* class and the range on the corresponding class whose subclasses and instances can possibly fill its range.

3.3 Linguistic Information

Since linguistic information as e.g. grammatical gender, its case, or the part-of-speech of a word is needed for analyzing natural language texts, this information has to be modeled, as well, in the ECtoloG. Therefore, we integrated the LingInfo model (Buitelaar et al., 2006) into the ECtoloG.

LingInfo constitutes an ontological model that provides other ontologies with linguistic information for different languages, momentarily for English, French, and German. Main objective of this ontology is to provide a mapping between ontological concepts and lexical items. That is, that the possibility is offered to assign linguistic information as e.g. the orthographic term, its grammatical gender, its part-of-speech, stem etc. to classes and properties. For our purposes, the LingInfo ontology had to be converted from RDFS into OWL-DL format and then integrated into the ECtoloG. For that reason, a new subclass of *owl:class* was defined: *ClassWithLingInfo*. Instances of this metaclass are linked through the *linginfo* property to *LingInfo* classes. The *LingInfo* class is used to associate a term, a language, and morphosyntactic information to classes from the ground ontology; e.g. a class *CafeConstruction*, which is an instance of *ClassWithLingInfo,* from an ontology proper, can be associated through the property *linginfo* with *Café*, an instance of the class *LingInfo*. Thus, the information that the term is *German*, its part-of-speech is *noun* and its grammatical gender *neuter* is obtained.

Following this approach, our classes of lexical constructions were defined as subclasses of *ClassWithLingInfo,* being thereby provided with all the necessary linguistic information as defined above. The central challenge resulting from this approach is, that through the definition of a metaclass the ontological format is no longer OWL-DL but goes to OWL-Full which thwarts the employment of Description Logic reasoners. Reasoning will not stay computable and decidable. Future work will address this challenge by means of intertwining the LingInfo model with the ECtoloG grammar model in such a way, that the computational and inferential properties of OWL-DL remain unchallenged.

Another possibility could be obtaining linguistic information for lexical items through an external lexicon.

4 The Web as a Corpus

The Seed Corpus *C:* The primary corpus *C* in this work is the portion of the World Wide Web confined to web pages containing natural language texts on soccer. To extract natural language texts out of web documents automatically we are using wrapper agents that fulfil this job (see Porzel et al., 2006). Our first goal is to build a grammar that can deal with all occurring language phenomena – i.e. both holophrastic and compositional ones – contained in that corpus *C*.

Corpus *C':* Next step is the development of a corpus C', where $C' = C + \varepsilon$ and ε is constituted by a set of new documents. This new corpus is not designed in an arbitrary manner. We search similar pages, adding add them to our original corpus *C*, as we expect the likelihood of still pretty good coverage together with some new constructions to be maximal, thereby enabling our incremental learning approach. The question emerging hereby is: what constitutes a similar web page? What, therefore, has to be explored are various similarity metrics, defining similarity in a concrete way and evaluate the results against human annotations (see Papineni et al., 2002).

4.1 Similarity Metric

To be able to answer the question which texts are actually similar, similarity needs to be defined precisely. Different approaches could be employed, i.e. regarding similarity in terms of syntactic or semantic phenomena or a combination of both. Since construction grammar makes no separation between syntax and semantics, phenomena that should be counted are both constructions and image schemas. As for holophrastic constructions this presents less of a challenge, we rather expect counting compositional ones being a 'tough cookie'.

To detect image schemas in natural text automatically, we seek to employ different methodologies, e.g. LSA (Kintsch and van Dijk, 1978), using synonym sets (Fellbaum, 1998) or other ontologies, which could assist in discovering the semantics of an unknown word with its corresponding schematic roles and the appropriate fillers. This or a similar methodology will be applied in the automatic acquisition process as well.

Another important point is that some terms, or some constructions, need to get a higher relevance factor than others, which will highly depend on context. Such a relevance factor can rank terms or constructions according to their importance in the respective text. Ranking functions that can be examined are, e.g., the TF/IDF function (e.g. Salton, 1989) or other so called *bag of words* approaches.

Term statistics in general is often used to determine a scalable measure of similarity between documents so it is said to be a good measure for topical closeness. Also part-of-speech statistics could be partly helpful in defining similarity of documents based on the ensuing type/token ratio.

The following five steps need to be executed in determining the similarity of two documents:

Step 1: Processing of the document D; analyzing the text and creating a list of all occurring words, constructions and/or image schemas. We assume that the best choice is counting constructions and corresponding image schemas, since they represent the semantics of the given text.

Step 2: Weighing of schemas and constructions

Step 3: Processing of the document D+1; executing of step 1 and 2 for this document.

Step 4: Comparing the documents; possibly adding synonyms of sources as e.g. WordNet (Fellbaum, 1998).

Step 5: Calculating the documents' similarity; defining a threshold up to which documents are considered as being similar. If a document is said to be similar, it is added to the corpus, which becomes the new corpus *C'*.

Analysis of the New Corpus C': The new corpus *C'* is analyzed, whereby the coverage results in coverage *A* of *C'* where:

$$A = 100\% - (\delta_h + \delta_c)$$

δ_h denotes all the holophrastic phenomena and δ_c all compositional phenomena not observed in *C*.

5 Grammar Learning

To generate a grammar that covers this new corpus *C'* different strategies have to be applied for holophrastic items δ_h which are lexical constructions in our approach and for compositional ones δ_c – meaning constructions on a higher level of abstraction as e.g. constructions that capture grammatical phenomena such as noun phrases or even whole sentences.

5.1 Learning Lexical Constructions

Analogous to the fast mapping process (Carey, 1978) of learning new words based on exposure without additional training or feedback on the correctness of its meaning, we are employing a method of filling our ontology with whole paradigms of new terms[8], enabled through the modeling of constructions described in 3.1. First step herein is employing a tool – Morphy (Lezius, 2002) – that enables morphological analysis and synthesis. The analysis of a term yields information about its stem, its part-of-speech, its case, its number, and its grammatical gender. This information can then easily be integrated automatically into the ECtoloG.

As already mentioned in section 4.3, we are not only trying to automatically acquire the form pole of the constructions, but also its image schematic meaning, that means the network of the schemas that hierarchically form the meaning pole of such a term, applying ontology learning mechanisms (e.g. Loos, 2006) and methods similar to those described in section 4.3. Additionally, investigations are underway to connect the grammar learning framework proposed herein to a computer vision system that provides supplementary feedback con-

[8] We are aware of the fact that fast mapping in humans is limited to color terms, shapes or texture terms, but are employing the method on other kinds of terms, nevertheless, since the grammar learning paradigm in our approach is still in its baby shoes.

cerning the hypothesized semantics of individual forms in the case of multi-media information.

5.2 Learning Compositional Constructions

Learning of compositional constructions still presents an issue which has not been accounted for, yet. What has already been proposed (Narayanan, inter alia) is that we have to assume a strong inductive bias and different learning algorithms, as e.g. some form of Bayesian learning or model merging (Stolcke, 1994) or reinforcement learning (Sutton and Barto, 1998).

Another important step that has to be employed is the (re)organization of the so-called constructicon, i.e. our inventory of constructions and schemas. These need to be merged, split or maybe thrown out again, depending on their utility, similarity etc.

5.3 Ambiguity

Currently the problem of ambiguity is solved by endowing the analyzer with a chart and employing the semantic density algorithm described in (Bryant, 2004). In the future probabilistic reasoning frameworks as proposed by (Narayanan and Jurafsky, 2005) in combination with ontology-based coherence measures as proposed by (Loos and Porzel, 2004) constitute promising approaches for handling problems of construal, whether it be on a pragmatic, semantic, syntactic or phonological level.

6 Concluding Remarks

In this paper we described our ongoing work in and thoughts on developing a grammar learning system based on a construction grammar formalism used in a question-answering system. We described necessary modules and presented first results and challenges in formalizing construction grammar. Furthermore, we pointed out our motivation for choosing construction grammar and the, therefore, resulting advantages. Then our approach and ideas of learning new linguistic phenomena, ranging from holophrastic constructions to compositional ones, were presented. What should be kept in mind is that our grammar model has to be strongly adaptable to language phenomena, as e.g. language variation and change, maps, metaphors, or mental spaces.

Evaluations in the light of the precision/coverage trade-off still present an enormous challenge (as with all adaptive and learning systems). In the future we will examine the feasibility of adapting ontology evaluating frameworks, as e.g. proposed by Porzel and Malaka (2005) for the task of grammar learning. We hope that future evaluations will show that our resulting system and, therefore, its grammar will be robust and adaptable enough to be worth being called 'Grammar Right'.

References

Allen, J.F. 1983. Maintaining Knowledge about Temporal Intervals. *Communications of the ACM, 26(11).*

Bergen, B. and Chang, N. 2002. Simulation-Based Language Understanding in Embodied Construction Grammar. ICSI TR-02-004, Berkeley, CA, USA.

Bryant, J. 2004. Recovering coherent interpretations using semantic integration of partial parses. *Proceedings of the 3rd ROMAND workshop*, Geneva, Switzerland.

Buitelaar, P., Declerck, T., Frank, A., Racioppa, S., Kiesel, M., Sintek, M., Engel, M., Romanelli, M., Sonntag, D., Loos, B., Micelli, V., Porzel, R. and Cimiano, P. 2006. LingInfo: Design and Applications of a Model for the Integration of Linguistic Information in Ontologies. *Proceedings of OntoLex 2006.* In Press. Genoa, Italy.

Bybee, J. 1998. A functionalist approach to grammar and its evolution. *Evolution of Communication 2(2).*

Carey, S. 1978. The child as word-learner. *Linguistic theory and psychological reality.* MIT Press, Cambridge, MA.

Chang, N., Feldman, J., Porzel, R. and Sanders, K. 2002. Scaling Cognitive Linguistics: Formalisms for Language Understanding. *Proceedings of the 1st ScaNaLU Workshop*, Heidelberg, Germany.

Chomsky, N. 1965. *Aspects of the theory of syntax.* MIT Press. Cambridge, Mass.

Croft, W. To appear. Logical and typological arguments for Radical Construction Grammar. *Construction Grammar(s): Cognitive and cross-language dimensions (Constructional approaches to Language, 1).* John Benjamins, Amsterdam.

Diessel, H. 2004. The Acquisition of Complex Sentences. *Cambridge Studies in Linguistics (105).* Cambridge University Press, Cambridge.

EDU: *Even Deeper Understanding* http://www.eml-development.de/english/research/edu/index.php (last access: 31/03/06).

Fellbaum, C. 1998. *WordNet: An Electronic Lexical Database*. MIT Press, Cambridge, Mass.

Fillmore, C. and Kay, P. 1987. The goals of Construction Grammar. *Berkeley Cognitive Science Program TR 50*. University of California, Berkeley.

Gallese, V. and Lakoff, G. 2005. The brain's concepts: the role of the sensory-motor system in conceptual knowledge. *Cognitive Neuropsychology 21/2005*.

Gangemi A., Mika P. 2003. Understanding the Semantic Web through Descriptions and Situations. *Proceedings of ODBASE03 Conference*, Springer.

Goldberg, A. 1995. *Constructions: A Construction Grammar Approach to Argument Structure*. University of Chicago Press. Chicago.

Guarino, N. 2006. Ontology Library. WonderWeb Deliverable D202, I STC-CNR, Padova, Italy. www.loa-cnr.it/Papers/Deliverable%202.pdf (last access: 31/03/2006).

Hopper, P. and Traugott, E. 2003. *Grammaticalization*. Cambridge University Press. Cambridge, UK.

Johnson, M. 1987. *The Body in the Mind: The Bodily Basis of Meaning, Imagination, and Reason*. University of Chicago Press. Chicago.

Katz, J. J. 1972. *Semantic theory*. Harper & Row. New York.

Kay, P. 2002. An Informal Sketch of a Formal Architecture for Construction Grammar. *Grammars 1/5*.

Kintsch, W. and van Dijk, T. 1978. Toward a model of text comprehension and production. *Psychological Review, 85 (5)*.

Lakoff, G. and Johnson, M. 1980. *Metaphors We Live By*. Chicago University Press. London.

Lakoff, G. 1987. *Women, Fire, and Dangerous Things*. University of Chicago Press. Chicago and London.

Langacker, R. 1987. *Foundations of Cognitive Grammar, Vol. 1*. University Press. Stanford.

Lezius, W. 2000. Morphy - German Morphology, Part-of-Speech Tagging and Applications. *Proceedings of the 9th EURALEX International Congress*, Stuttgart, Germany.

Loos, B. 2006. Scaling natural language understanding via user-driven ontology learning. *This volume*.

Loos, B. and Porzel, R. 2004. Resolution of Lexical Ambiguities in Spoken Dialogue System. *Proceedings of the 5th SIGdial Workshop on Discourse and Dialogue*, Cambridge, Massachusetts, USA.

Masolo, C., Borgo, S., Gangemi, A., Guarino, N., and Oltramari, A. 2003. Ontology Library. WonderWeb Deliverable D18, I STC-CNR, Padova, Italy. http://wonderweb.semanticweb.org/deliverables/documents/D18.pdf.

Micelli, V., Porzel, R., and Gangemi, A. In Press. ECtoloG: Construction Grammar meets the Semantic Web. *Proceedings of ICCG4*, Tokyo, Japan.

Narayanan, S. and Jurafsky, D. 2005. *A Bayesian Model of Human Sentence Processing* (in preparation).

Narayanan, S. 2006. Lecture Series given at Interdisciplinary College, Guenne, Lake Moehne, March 10th – 17th.

NTL: *Neural Theory of Language* http://www.icsi.berkeley.edu/NTL/

Papineni, K., Roukos, S., Ward, T. and Zhu, W. 2002. Bleu: a Method for Automatic Evaluation of Machine Translation. *Proceedings of the 40th Annual Meeting of the Association for Computational Linguistics (ACL)*, Philadelphia.

Porzel, R. and Malaka, R. 2005. A Task-based Framework for Ontology Learning, Population and Evaluation. Ontology Learning from Text: Methods, Evaluation and Applications Frontiers. *Artificial Intelligence and Applications Series, Vol. 123*, IOS Press.

Porzel, R., Micelli, V., Aras, H., and Zorn, H.-P. 2006. Tying the Knot: Ground Entities, Descriptions and Information Objects for Construction-based Information Extraction. *Proceedings of OntoLex 2006*. In Press. Genoa, Italy.

Salton, G. 1989. *Automatic Text Processing: the Transformation, Analysis, and Retrieval of Information by Computer*. Addison-Wesley. Reading, MA.

Steels, L. 2005. The Role of Construction Grammar in Fluid Language Grounding. Submitted. Elsevier Science.

Stolcke, A. 1994. Bayesian Learning of Probabilistic Language Models. *Ph.D. Thesis*, Computer Science Division, University of California at Berkeley.

Sutton, R. and Barto, A. 1998. *Reinforcement Learning: An Introduction*. MIT Press, Cambridge.

Talmy, L. 1988. Force dynamics in language and cognition. *Cognitive Science, 12*.

Tomasello, M. 2003. *Constructing a Language: A Usage-Based Theory of Language Acquisition*. Harvard University Press.

Embodied construction grammar as layered modal languages

Anders Søgaard
Center for Language Technology
Njalsgade 80
DK-2300 Copenhagen
anders@cst.dk

Abstract

One can think of scalability in terms of complexity or granularity, but in both cases, modal languages seem to be of interest: Modal languages are robustly decidable, and they encode in a natural way the idea of refinement by layering, which implies scalability in terms of granularity. The contribution of this paper is to introduce the general technique of translating problems of scalable natural language understanding into layered modal languages; for illustration, a translation is sketched for Embodied Construction Grammar (ECG). On the basis of this translation, an upper bound on the complexity of ECG is established: the universal recognition problem of ECG is solvable in EXPTIME (if some dynamic resetting is assumed). If the use of the **evokes**-operator is polynomially bound, the recognition problem turns NP-complete.

1 Introduction

The purpose of this paper is to demonstrate that problems of scalable natural understanding translate into layered modal languages. Since the properties of such languages are well-studied, such a translation is an important achievement. In this paper, this is illustrated by providing a translation from ECG into a layered extension of modal logic with nominals from which complexity results can be derived. On the general note, ECG is a step in the direction of a formal specification and interpretation of various theories proposed in the cognitive linguistics community. Many questions pop up with the introduction of such a theory, for instance: Does ECG faithfully reflect the intuitions of the original proposals, e.g. mental space theory (see below)? Can it be implemented on existing grammar engineering platforms? What is its computational complexity? Etc. Some of these questions are answered in this paper, some are not; in particular, we do not examine the "faithfullness" of ECG to the original sources. Our purpose here is to investigate its computational properties. This purpose is, however, in the author's view, secondary to the introduction of layered modal languages as a method for scalable natural language understanding. Let us first begin with some technicalities, a simple example of a layered modal language:

Example 1.1. Consider a propositional modal logic ($\mathcal{L}$) of two domains $\mathbb{D}$ and $\mathbb{E}$ and $\mathbb{D} \cap \mathbb{E} = \emptyset$. $\mathbb{D}$ and $\mathbb{E}$ are nodes in a Kripke model $\langle \mathcal{W}, \mathcal{R}, \mathcal{V} \rangle$ (worlds, relations, valuation), s.t. $\mathcal{W} \subseteq \mathbb{D} \cup \mathbb{E}$. Let δ and ϵ be propositions. Say δ in the model denotes a subset of $\mathbb{D}$, i.e. $[\![\delta]\!] \subseteq \mathbb{D}$, and ϵ denotes a subset of $\mathbb{E}$. Consider the axioms $\delta \vee \epsilon$, $\neg(\delta \wedge \epsilon)$, and $\langle \tau \rangle \phi \rightarrow \delta \wedge \langle \tau \rangle (\epsilon \wedge \phi)$, formulated in $\mathcal{L}$. The first two axioms ensure that $\mathbb{D}$ and $\mathbb{E}$ are disjoint and exhaustive, and the last axiom ensures that $R_\tau \in \mathcal{R}$ is a transition relation from $\mathbb{D}$ to $\mathbb{E}$. Call this language $\mathcal{L}^{\mathbb{D},\mathbb{E}}$. $\mathcal{L}^{\mathbb{D},\mathbb{E}}$ is a language with a complex ontology, i.e. it distinguishes between two disjoint domains.

Proceedings of the 3rd Workshop on Scalable Natural Language Understanding, pages 65–72,
New York City, June 2006.

On the logical side, the paper is about layered modal languages with rich ontologies. A language is introduced that extends $\mathcal{L}$ in a number of respects, e.g. it is both hybrid and dynamic. If the reader has no idea about the nature of such a language in advance, please have patience. The language is formally defined below. It is used to encode ECG, a complex theory of natural language understanding that comprises several domains. In fact, the ontology of ECG is further extended here with an inference component. This is the second advantage of our translation, besides from the complexity results: Since layering is fully scalable, it is easy to integrate ECG with a database of real-world knowledge and inference components. The inference component really refers to a structured set of subdomains, incl. a referential, spatial and a temporal subdomain. On the historical note, the layering techniques, as they are employed here, were introduced, in a systematic way, in the logic community by Blackburn and de Rijke (1997), but see references therein for earlier applications of the techniques. It is of course also possible to layer fundamentally different logics.

The structure of the paper is simple: The second section introduces our modal language and its expressivity. The language is, on arbitrary frames, decidable in deterministic exponential time (Areces et al., 1999, Theorem 3.5), and equivalent to propositional dynamic logic with converse, enriched with nominals and global modalities. The next section is a brief presentation of ECG and its translation into our layered modal language. In the fourth section, the complexity results are established. The results are conjectured to transfer to related linguistic formalisms. Our results also indicate that ECG can be implemented on common grammar engineering platforms, and an implementation is sketched for the Lexical Knowledge Base (Copestake, 2001). Finally, a modal language of greater expressivity (and higher complexity) is considered.

2 Logic

Our language is, as mentioned, a dynamic and hybrid extension of modal logic, but not only that. It extends $\mathcal{L}$ with nominals (propositions that denote singleton subsets), satisfaction operators, global modalities, non-deterministic operators and the converse operator. Call the language ScU.

Definition 2.1. In ScU, formulas are built over a set of propositions $\mathbb{PROP}$, denoted by $\{p, q, \ldots\}$ or type names such as *word* or *phrase*, and a set of nominals $\mathbb{NOM}$, denoted by $\{i, j, \ldots\}$, s.t.

$$\phi := p|i|\neg\phi|\phi \vee \psi|\langle\alpha\rangle\phi|@_i\phi|\langle\alpha^{-1}\rangle\phi|\langle\alpha^*\rangle\phi|A\phi$$

are wellformed. The satisfaction definition is as follows, wrt. Kripke models $\langle\mathcal{W}, \mathcal{R}, \mathcal{V}\rangle$, where $\mathcal{W}$ is a set of worlds, $\mathcal{R}$ a set of binary relations, and $\mathcal{V}$ is the valuation function, i.e. a mapping from $\mathbb{PROP}$ and $\mathbb{NOM}$ to the power set of $\mathcal{W}$:

$M, w \models p$	iff	$w \in \mathcal{V}(p)$
$M, w \models i$	iff	$\mathcal{V}(i) = \{w\}$
$M, w \models \neg\phi$	iff	$M, w \not\models \phi$
$M, w \models \phi \vee \psi$	iff	$M, w \models \phi$ or $M, w \models \psi$
$M, w \models \langle\alpha\rangle\phi$	iff	$\exists w'(R_\alpha(w, w')\& M, w' \models \phi)$
$M, w \models @_i\phi$	iff	$M, w' \models \phi\&\mathcal{V}(i) = \{w'\}$
$M, w \models \langle\alpha^{-1}\rangle\phi$	iff	$\exists w'(R_\alpha^{-1}(w, w')\& M, w' \models \phi)$
$M, w \models \langle\alpha^*\rangle\phi$	iff	$\exists w'(wR_\alpha^* w'\ \&\ M, w' \models \phi)$
$M, w \models A\phi$	iff	$\forall w'\ M, w' \models \phi$

where R_α^* means $\bigcup_n (R_\alpha)^n$, and n is non-deterministically chosen, and where R_α^{-1} is the converse of R_α.

For abbreviatory use, ;, $\cup$ are defined s.t.

;: $\langle\alpha\rangle\langle\beta\rangle\phi \leftrightarrow \langle\alpha; \beta\rangle\phi$

$\cup$: $\langle\alpha\rangle\phi \vee \langle\beta\rangle\phi \leftrightarrow \langle\alpha \cup \beta\rangle\phi$

(The next paragraphs motivate the various operators of ScU *and chacterizes its expressivity, in part. If the reader is unaccustomed to the literature on modal languages, the paragraphs may be somewhat dense, and she is invited to skip the rest of this section.)* Our extensions of $\mathcal{L}$ by nominals, satisfaction operators, global modalities, non-deterministic operators and the converse operator are meaningful, as evidenced by an investigation of the invariance properties of ScU. If a logic is invariant under some operation, you may recall, it means that it preserves

validities under this operation, and that properties that are affected by it, cannot be defined. $\mathcal{L}$ is characterized in part by its invariance under disjoint unions, bounded morphisms and bisimulation. Briefly put, if a logic is invariant under disjoint unions, it means that any validities that hold for some model M, also hold in the disjoint union $M \uplus M'$ for any model M'. A bounded morphism h ensures that for every $w \in \mathcal{W}$, w and $h(w)$ satisfy the same proposition letters, h is a homomorphism wrt. the relations in $\mathcal{R}$ (the forth condition), and for every $R \in \mathcal{R}$, if $R'h(w)w'$, then there exists w'' s.t. Rww'' and $h(w'') = w'$ (the back condition) (Blackburn et al., 2001, 59). A bisimulation between (unimodal) models $M = \langle \mathcal{W}, R, \mathcal{V} \rangle$ and $M' = \langle \mathcal{W}', R', \mathcal{V}' \rangle$ is a non-empty binary relation Z between their points s.t. whenever wZw' we have that:

(i) w and w' satisfy the same proposition symbols,

(ii) if Rvw, then there exists a point $v' \in M'$ s.t. vZv' and $R'w'v'$, and

(iii) if $R'v'w'$, then there exists a point $v \in M$ s.t. vZv' and Rwv.

This generalizes straight-forwardly to the polymodal case. ScU is not invariant under any of these operations. Invariance under disjoint unions is lost, once you add global modalities. This is obvious, since global modalities allow you to say, for instance, "there is no state in ϕ". This may hold true for M, but not for M', and thus not for $M \uplus M'$ either. ScU clearly encodes hybrid logic ($\mathcal{H}$), which is defined as the extension of $\mathcal{L}$ with nominals and satisfaction operators. Since $\mathcal{H}$ is non-invariant under bounded morphisms (ten Cate, 2005), the non-invariance of ScU follows. The notion of bisimulation, finally, does not take nominals into account. The operation can be modified a bit, however. The bisimulation operation for $\mathcal{H}$, call it $\mathcal{H}$-bisimulation, adds a fourth clause to its definition, namely that

(iv) all points named by nominals are related by Z.

In addition, clause (i) takes $\mathbb{NOM} \cup \mathbb{PROP}$ as its domain, rather than just $\mathbb{PROP}$. Unfortunately, this is not enough. The global modalities force us to add a fifth requirement, namely that the operation is total, i.e. s.t. $\forall \nu_i \in W\ \exists \nu_j \in W'\ \nu_i Z \nu_j$, and vice versa. The obvious reason is that global modalities are sensitive to information in non-local (disconnected) substructures. Call this total bisimulation for $\mathcal{H}(E)$-bisimulation (ten Cate, 2005, 47).

Lemma 2.2. ScU *is invariant under* $\mathcal{H}(E)$-*bisimulation.*

Proof. This follows from the invariance of $\mathcal{H}$ extended with global modalities ($\mathcal{H}(E)$) under $\mathcal{H}(E)$-bisimulation (ten Cate, 2005), and that $*$ and -1 are safe for $\mathcal{H}(E)$-bisimulation. Van Benthem (1998) proved that $*$ is safe for bisimulation. Consequently, if Z is a bisimulation from $M = \langle \mathcal{W}, R, \mathcal{V} \rangle$ to $M' = \langle \mathcal{W}', R', \mathcal{V}' \rangle$, it is also a bisimulation between $M = \langle \mathcal{W}, R^*, \mathcal{V} \rangle$ and $M' = \langle \mathcal{W}', (R')^*, \mathcal{V}' \rangle$. If Z is a $\mathcal{H}(E)$-bisimulation it also satisfies the fourth clause of the definition above, i.e. all points named by nominals are related by Z, and it must have a full domain and range (be total). These properties are not dependent on the transition relations, however, since they only depend on the domains and valuations of the models. $*$ is thus safe for $\mathcal{H}(E)$-bisimulation too. The safety of the converse operator -1 follows from the equivalence of $\mathcal{H}(E)$-bisimulation and so-called power bisimulation, introduced recently by van Benthem for a logic of games. Since this logic included -1 and was invariant under power bisimulation, it follows that -1 is also safe for $\mathcal{H}(E)$-bisimulation. □

It can be inferred from the non-invariance of $\mathcal{H}$ under bounded morphism that the extension of $\mathcal{L}$ by nominals and satisfaction operators is meaningful, while the non-invariance under disjoint union tells us that global modalities also add expressive power to our language. The extension of $\mathcal{L}$ by non-deterministic operators is meaningful too, evidenced by the loss of compactness (Blackburn et al., 2001, 240). (Since $\mathcal{L}$ has a translation into first order logic, it is compact.) Converse, finally, is also meaningful. Consider, for instance, the model $\{R^{-1}(w, w')\}$, which cannot be singled out by any $\mathcal{L}$ or propositional dynamic formula.

Note that ScU, unlike $\mathcal{L}$, does *not* have the tree model property, i.e. it is not the case that ϕ is satisfiable iff it is satisfiable in a tree-like Kripke model. This is important, since the grammar formalisms considered here all employ reentrancies, a property that violates the tree model property. In other words, if ScU had the tree model property, it would not be able to encode or reconstruct the formalisms this paper concerns.

3 Grammar

The fundamental concept in ECG is that of feature structures. The reader is invited to think of such feature structures as Kripke structures. On this view, with some mild abuse of notation, it holds that, for instance,

$$\begin{bmatrix} \text{FUNCT} & \begin{bmatrix} \text{NUM} & \boxed{1} \end{bmatrix} \\ \text{ARG} & \begin{bmatrix} \text{NUM} & \boxed{1} \end{bmatrix} \end{bmatrix}$$

$$\models \langle \text{FUNCT} \rangle \langle \text{NUM} \rangle i \wedge \langle \text{ARG} \rangle \langle \text{NUM} \rangle i$$

The tags are used to "co-index" two values. Consequently, they denote reentrancies. In ScU, tags translate into nominals, since they denote singleton sets of states. The standard ECG notation look different from standard attribute-value matrices, but to a large extent the schemas of ECG can be viewed as notational variants of Kripke structures. For instance,

schema Trajector-Landmark **subcase of** Image-Schema **roles** trajector: *a* landmark: *b*

is equivalent to

$$\begin{bmatrix} \textit{trajector\_landmark} & \\ \text{ROLES} & \begin{bmatrix} \text{TRAJECTOR} & a \\ \text{LANDMARK} & b \end{bmatrix} \end{bmatrix}$$

$$\wedge \textit{trajector\_landmark} \sqsupseteq \textit{image\_schema}$$

The last formula says that *trajector_landmark* is a subtype of *image_schema*. The root node is thus in the denotation of both propositions. The *trajector_landmark* type is a schema. Schemas and constructions constitute two different domains in ECG. Schemas, in general, encode conceptual structure and constrain information about conceptual roles and the relations among them. Constructions are linguistic of nature and pair up form and meaning (two subdomains identified by separate attributes). The third domain is that of spaces. The ontology, summarized here, is presented in more detail in Chang et al. (2002). Let *schema* denote the domain of schemas, *constr* denote the domain of constructions, while *ms* denotes the domain of (mental) spaces. The domain structure is defined in the same way as in Example 1.1. A map modality is also introduced; this is used to encode the **map**-operator, also introduced in Chang et al. (2002), which is said to identify "correspondences across a pair of conceptual domains (e.g. between two schemas, or between two spaces)."

(1) $schema \vee constr \vee ms$

(2) $\neg(schema \wedge constr \vee schema \wedge ms \vee constr \wedge ms$

(3) $\langle map \rangle \phi \rightarrow (schema \wedge \langle map \rangle (schema \wedge \phi)) \vee (ms \wedge \langle map \rangle (ms \wedge \phi))$

Reentrancies are denoted by $\leftrightarrow$. In other words,

a $\leftrightarrow$ b

corresponds to

$$\begin{bmatrix} \text{A} & \boxed{1} \\ \text{B} & \boxed{1} \end{bmatrix}$$

Feature structures, more generally, are governed by a number of axioms; see for instance Wedekind (1997). Feature structures have (mostly) deterministic attributes, and they are acyclic, connected and rooted. This can be encoded in ScU in this way, if *root* is a nominal:

(4) $\langle \alpha \rangle i \rightarrow [\alpha] i$ (functionality)

(5) $i \rightarrow \neg \langle \alpha_1 \cup \cdots \cup \alpha_n \rangle^+ i$ (acyclicity)

(6) $E(root \wedge \neg \langle \alpha^{-1} \rangle \top) \wedge A(\langle \alpha_1 \cup \cdots \cup \alpha_n \rangle^* root)$ (connectedness and rootedness)

R_α is, as in the above, any relation in $\mathcal{R}$, $\mathcal{R} = \{\alpha_1 \dots \alpha_n\}$, and axioms are multiplied in the set of nominals.

Up to this point, ECG looks exactly like other unification-based formalisms (the feature geometry and its linguistic use aside). ECG employs two novel operators, however; most significantly, the so-called **evokes** operator, which triggers a new schema and allows reference to it. In ScU, this corresponds to existential quantification and naming, e.g.

schema s **evokes** t **as** i **roles** k ↔ i.l	**schema** t **roles** l : a

$$\models s \wedge \langle k \rangle j \wedge E(i \wedge \langle l \rangle (a \wedge j))$$

The other complication is the "::" constraints. Since this constraint involves quantification over times, it is discussed in the section on inference just below, where a temporal domain is introduced.

ECG usually employs rather flat constructions, and linearization can be constrained in two ways: either by weak or immediate precedence (Bryant, 2004). We use standard terminology and let $\prec$ denote weak precedence and $\ll$ denote immediate precedence. It is an option to augment the ECG feature geometry with a domain of substructures for phonological strings (distinguished by a feature PHON, for instance). The standard encoding of lists as trees can be employed, and ScU used to constrain the tree structures. One can, alternatively, represent strings by linear relations. This is the solution adopted here. This is possible if the input to the parsing procedure is the lexical entries rather than the strings themselves. It is of course trivial to do this substitution (lexical ambiguity just blows up the number of inputs). $\prec$ and $\ll$ are then interpreted directly over substructures (or type propositions, really), i.e. $\ll$ is a deterministic version of the $\prec$ modality s.t.

(7) $\prec \phi \Leftrightarrow \ll^+ \phi$

Mental space theory, originally due to Gilles Fauconnier, is used as a semantic representation language in an extension of ECG proposed by Mok et al. (2004). The implementation suggested there does not increase the formal complexity of ECG. It only extends the feature geometry. A separate domain for spaces was already introduced.

We are now in a position to show how ECG analysis works, and more importantly, a parsing procedure is identified. Contrary to the parsing procedure hinted at in (Bryant, 2004), this algorithm is entirely model-theoretic. The toy implementation presented below is comparable to Bryant's proposal, in that the Lexical Knowledge Base employs generative rules in a bottom-up fashion. The basics of our parsing procedure is:

1. The string is encoded in ScU and conjoined with the axioms of ECG.

2. If this conjoined formula is satisfiable, the string is accepted.

It is easy to represent strings in our language, as already indicated. The job is to identify the proper axioms. Some were already defined, i.e. (1-7). It is now necessary to define the type hierarchy, which includes the various types of schemas, constructions, and spaces. It is also necessary to define some start or root type, which is existentially quantified over. Why is that? This is to ensure that all the relevant information is derived in the parse. The definition of the type hierarchy, and total well-typing in particular (Carpenter, 1992), is half the way, but it is necessary to ensure, somehow, that the model which satisfies the string is forced to contain a full linguistic analysis (and not just the empty model or some arbitrary connection of the constituent substructures derived from the lexicon). This is easily obtained by existential quantification over the root and connectivity. If there is a root and a set of constituent substructures, and the feature structure has to be connected, the additional structure falls out by implications. It is necessary, however, since this is a typed system, to ensure that the "universal" phrase, i.e. the supertype *phrase*, cannot apply. In generative or rule-based systems, such as the

Lexical Knowledge Base, this is ensured by stipulating directly which types count as rules. On a model-theoretic set-up, it is necessary to add some implication that every phrase is a particular type of phrase.[1]

3.1 Inference

To this we add an inference component. The inference component has a complex structure and comprises multiple subdomains. Only three domains are included here, for simplicity. The domains include a referential (R), a spatial (S), and a temporal one (T). The transitions are called R_{r2s}, from the referential to the spatial domain, and R_{s2t}, from the spatial to the temporal domain. The domains are denoted by propositions *ref*, *space* and *time*.

Example 3.1. Our layering is illustrated by this simple example:

(8) The new teacher enters the room in a minute.

Think of the room as a spatial region that the teacher at some point (in time) is part of. t_0 is the time of the utterance.

$$\begin{array}{ll} & E(time \wedge t_1 \wedge @_{t_0}\langle 60s\rangle t_1) \\ \wedge & E(space \wedge i \wedge \leq room \wedge @_i\langle s2t\rangle t_1) \\ \wedge & E(ref \wedge \langle new\rangle(teacher \wedge \langle r2s\rangle i)) \end{array}$$

The model that satisfies the formula will look like this:

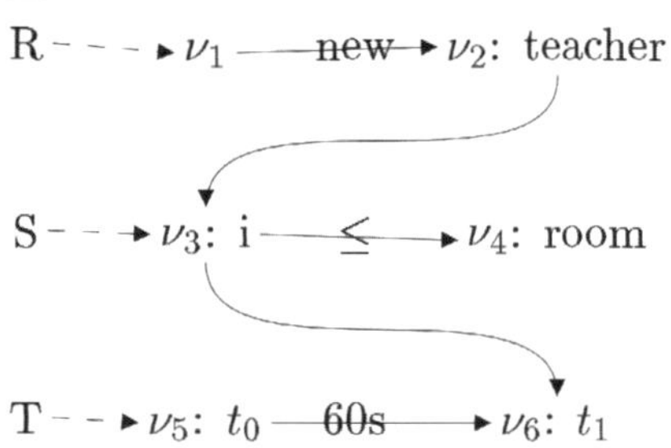

Here R is the referential domain, S is the spatial domain, and T is the temporal one. The curved lines are the projections from one domain to another, i.e. R_{r2s} and R_{s2t}. The R domain says that there is a teacher who is new. The S domain says that his spatial instantiation is part of the spatial region that is occupied by the room at time t_1. The T domain tells us that t_1 is 60 seconds from now.

Remark 3.2. A remark on the :: constraints of ECG was promised you. In Chang et al. (2002, Figure 2), two such constraints are used to say that in the schema "Translational-Motion", the mover's location changes from that of the source to that of the goal at the time of the motion, i.e. because of the motion. Call this temporal state t_m. The constraints

```
...
  before :: mover.location ↔ source
  after :: mover.location ↔ goal
```

thus translate into

$$A(\langle<\rangle t_m \rightarrow \langle s2t^{-1}\rangle source) \text{ and}$$
$$A(\langle>\rangle t_m \rightarrow \langle s2t^{-1}\rangle goal)$$

4 Computational issues

`ScU` is decidable in deterministic exponential time (Areces et al., 1999, Theorem 3.5). It follows from the parsing procedure and the completeness of our translation that so is ECG. If the inference component is ignored, the **evokes**-free fragment of ECG is apparently more efficient, since an NP-completeness result can be established for it. Obtaining the result is not too complicated. The domain minimal Kripke model that satisfies an input formula in these theories is bound by a size lemma. ECG contains no unary constructions (as it is shown below, **evokes** does the job of unary projections), but such can be freely added, provided that unary rules only apply once to the same unary extension. If a unary extension is always the result of a single application of a unary rule, $u = 1$.

Lemma 4.1. *A* `ScU` *formula that encodes a recognition problem for the* **evokes***-free fragment of ECG for some string* σ *is, if satisfiable, satisfied by a structure* M *of at most* $(2|\sigma| - 1)(u + 1) \times$ **paths** *cardinality, where* $2|\sigma| - 1$ *is the maximum number of nodes in a binary tree,* u *is the number of unary rules, and* **paths** *is the number of paths licensed by the non-recursive part of the feature geometry of ECG. In particular,* **paths** $= |\{\pi \in$ `Lbls`$^* |$ *no label occurs twice in* $\pi\}|$.

[1] This is roughly the role of the immediate dominance principle in head-driven phrase structure grammar.

Since any ScU formula ϕ that represents an **evokes**-free ECG recognition problem for a string of c length, can be evaluated in a model of size polynomial to c, a suitable model can be non-deterministically chosen, and ϕ is evaluated in polynomial time, since model checking in ScU and similar languages is decidable in polynomial time (Franceschet and de Rijke, 2006). It follows that

Theorem 4.2. *The universal recognition problem of **evokes**-free ECG is decidable in non-deterministic polynomial time.*

Remark 4.3. The result in Theorem 4.2 transfers to unification categorial grammar and construction grammar where u is bound in the same way.

4.1 Implementation

In this subsection, it is sketched how ECG, at least in part, can be implemented in the Lexical Knowledge Base (Copestake, 2001). This has already been hinted at in different places. The reader familiar with both the computational platform and the literature on ECG may envisage how to implement the **evokes**-free fragment. Consequently, we focus only on how to translate the **evokes** operator by unary rules. Lexical rules could also have been used, but lexical rules are rather heavy and unruly machineries, and they are best avoided if possible.

We consider the example from above. It holds that

schema s **evokes** t **as** i **roles** k ↔ i.l	**schema** t **roles** l : a	is equivalent to

$$\begin{bmatrix} s \\ \text{ROLES } \boxed{1} \\ \text{EVOKES } \begin{bmatrix} t \\ \text{ROLES } \begin{bmatrix} \text{L } \boxed{1} \end{bmatrix} \end{bmatrix} \end{bmatrix}$$

$$\begin{bmatrix} s \\ \text{ROLES } \boxed{1} \text{ a} \end{bmatrix}$$

The **evokes** operator is thus replaced by a recursive attribute which embeds the new structure. Since the EVOKES attribute is defined for this sole purpose, it is really no different from the disconnected substructure intended in the ECG-style notation. The other complication, the :: operator, deserves a brief remark too. If the relational constraints of the schemas are augmented with events, that is, each proposition is defined relative to some event (as in Davidsonian semantics), the ::-style constraints can be translated into ordinary relations. This extends the feature geometry a bit, of course, but enables us to implement ECG in the Lexical Knowledge Base.

4.2 Using a richer logic

There is one qualification to our formalization that has not been mentioned yet (except for in the abstract), namely that certain undesired reentrancies may appear in the context of the **evoke** operator (and schemas and constructions, more generally), if the nominals used in the reduction are not somehow dynamically reset. The intuition is this: If a schema runs an **evoke** operation, it existentially asserts a substructure and names some of its nodes by nominals. However, the next time this schema applies, the substructure in the scope of the operator, receives the same names, unless they are somehow changed (dynamically). It is possible to avoid this complication, if one "steps up" our logic a bit, i.e. if we add quantification over nominals. We are then able to quantify over both nominals and states. Call the relevant quantifier $\exists$. Its satisfaction definition is

$$M, g, w \models \exists x\ \phi \quad \text{iff} \quad \exists g'\ g \stackrel{c}{=} \& M, g', w \models \phi$$

Note that assignments have now been added to the satisfaction definitions, for obvious reasons. The standard translation into first order logic illustrates its intended meaning:

$$ST_x(\exists y\ \phi){=}\exists y\ ST_x(\phi)$$

Our logic now, with this new extension, embeds hybrid logic extended with the $\Downarrow$ operator,[2] and since this logic has been shown to be undecidable (Blackburn and Seligman, 1995), our logic is thus undecidable itself. However, NP-completeness can still be established for a useful

[2]This follows from the fact that $\Downarrow x\ \phi \doteq \downarrow x\ A(\phi)$.

fragment. The intuition behind the fragment is, as we saw in our computational implementation, that **evokes** operations are much like unary projections. Constraint-based grammars are often (only) undecidable in the abscence of off-line parsability constraints, and in fact an "off-line parsability" restriction can be placed on the use of the **evokes** operator. Simply label all the **evokes** operators employed in the schemas. Say that any schema that evokes a schema or space that evokes another one, etc., can never evoke itself in this chain of evocations. Call our new language $\texttt{ScU}^+$ and let **evocators** be the number of **evokes** operators employed by the grammar. Call the restriction on the use of **evokes** the "acyclic evocation restriction." The following size lemma now holds:[3]

Lemma 4.4. *A* $\texttt{ScU}^+$ *formula that encodes an ECG recognition problem for some string* σ *under the acyclic evocation restriction is, if satisfiable, satisfied by a structure M of at most* $(2|\sigma|-1)$**evocators** $\times$ **paths** *cardinality, where* **evocators** *and* **paths** *are defined as in the above.*

It follows as a corrollary that

Theorem 4.5. *The universal recognition problem of ECG under the acyclic evocation restriction is decidable in non-deterministic polynomial time.*

Proof. Similar to the proof of Theorem 4.2. □

5 Conclusions

The technique of using layered modal language for scalable natural language understanding was introduced and applied to ECG. Certain interesting results were derived. ECG is decidable in exponential time (under dynamic resetting), its **evokes**-free fragment is NP-complete, and so is ECG under the acyclic evocation restriction, i.e. if we put a bound on the length of evocations which is polynomial in the length of the input. It was also shown to be likely that ECG can be implemented in the Lexical Knowledge Base.

[3] It is, for simplification, assumed that each schema or space contains at most one **evokes** operator.

References

Carlos Areces, Patrick Blackburn, and Maarten Marx. 1999. A road-map on complexity for hybrid logics. In *Proceedings of the Annual Conference of the European Association for Computer Science Logic*, volume 1683 of *Lecture Notes in Computer Science*, pages 307–321, Berlin. Springer.

Patrick Blackburn and Maarten de Rijke. 1997. Zooming in, zooming out. *Journal of Logic, Language and Information*, 6:5–31.

Patrick Blackburn and Jerry Seligman. 1995. Hybrid languages. *Journal of Logic, Language and Information*, 4:251–272.

Patrick Blackburn, Maarten de Rijke, and Yde Venema. 2001. *Modal logic*. Cambridge University Press, Cambridge, England.

John Bryant. 2004. Scalable construction-based parsing and semantic analysis. Presented at Scalable Natural Language Understanding 2004.

Bob Carpenter. 1992. *The logic of typed feature structures*, volume 32 of *Cambridge Tracts in Theoretical Computer Science*. Cambridge University Press, Cambridge, England.

Nancy Chang, Jerome Feldman, Robert Porzel, and Keith Sanders. 2002. Scaling cognitive linguistiscs: formalisms for language understanding. Presented at Scalable Natural Language Understanding 2002.

Ann Copestake. 2001. *Implementing typed feature structure grammars*. CSLI, Stanford, California.

Massimo Franceschet and Maarten de Rijke. 2006. Model checking for hybrid logics. *Journal of Applied Logic*. In press.

Eva Mok, John Bryant, and Jerome Feldman. 2004. Scaling understanding up to mental spaces. Presented at Scalable Natural Language Understanding 2004.

Balder ten Cate. 2005. *Model theory for extended modal languages*. Ph.D. thesis, University of Amsterdam, Amsterdam, the Netherlands. ILLC Dissertation Series DS-2005-01.

Johan van Benthem. 1998. Program constructions that are safe for bisimulation. *Studia logica*, 60:311–330.

Jürgen Wedekind. 1997. Approaches to unification in grammar. In Patrick Blackburn and Maarten de Rijke, editors, *Specifying syntactic structure*, pages 245–280. CSLI Publications, Stanford, California.

A (very) Brief Introduction to Fluid Construction Grammar

Luc Steels(1,2) and Joachim de Beule(1)
(1) University of Brussels (VUB AI Lab)
(2) SONY Computer Science Lab - Paris
steels@arti.vub.ac.be

Abstract

Fluid Construction Grammar (FCG) is a new linguistic formalism designed to explore in how far a construction grammar approach can be used for handling open-ended grounded dialogue, i.e. dialogue between or with autonomous embodied agents about the world as experienced through their sensory-motor apparatus. We seek scalable, open-ended language systems by giving agents both the ability to use existing conventions or ontologies, and to invent or learn new ones as the needs arise. This paper contains a brief introduction to the key ideas behind FCG and its current status.

1 Introduction

Construction grammar is receiving growing attention lately, partly because it has allowed linguists to discuss a wide range of phenomena which were difficult to handle in earlier frameworks (Goldberg, 1995; OstmanFried, 2005; Croft, 2001), and partly because it has allowed psychologists to describe in a more satisfactory way early language development (TomaselloBrooks, 1999). There were already some attempts to formalise construction grammar (KayFillmore, 1999) and build a computational implementation (BergenChang, 2003), but many open problems remain and at this early stage of fundamental research, it makes sense to explore alternative approaches. In our team, we focus on open-ended grounded dialogue, in other words how it is possible for a speaker to formulate an utterance about the world and for a hearer to understand what is meant (ClarkBrennan, 1991). The present paper briefly reports on the formalisation of construction grammar called Fluid Construction Grammar (FCG) that we have developed for this research. Although the formalism is novel in several fundamental aspects, it also builds heavily on the state of the art in formal and computational linguistics, particularly within the tradition of unification-based feature structure grammars such as HPSG (PollardSag, 1994). FCG has been under development from around 2001 and an implementation on a LISP substrate has been released through http://arti.vub.ac.be/FCG/ in 2005. The FCG core engine (for parsing and production) is fully operational and has already been used in some large-scale experiments in language grounding (SteelsLoetzsch, 2006). We do not claim to have a complete solution for all linguistic issues that arise in construction grammar, and neither do we claim that the solutions we have adopted so far are final. On the contrary, we are aware of many difficult technical issues that still remain unresolved and welcome any discussion that would bring us forward.

2 Motivations

FCG grew out of efforts to understand the creative basis of language. Language creativity is more than the application of an existing set of rules (even if the rules are recursive and thus allow an infinite set of possible sentences). Human language users often stretch and expand rules whenever the need arises,

Proceedings of the 3rd Workshop on Scalable Natural Language Understanding, pages 73–80,
New York City, June 2006. ©c 2006 Association for Computational Linguistics

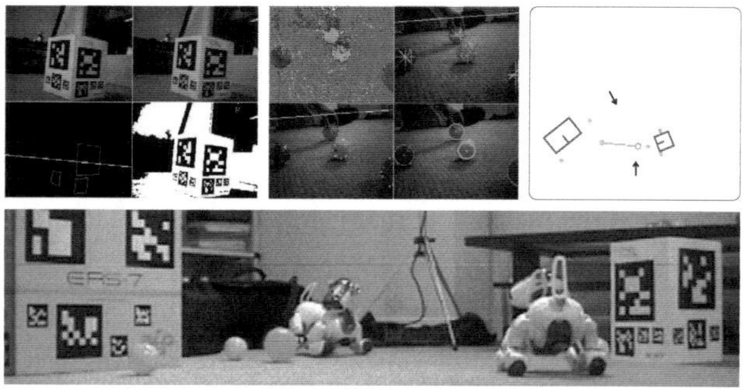

Figure 1: Typical experimental setup. The bottom shows two robots moving around in an environment that contains balls and boxes. The robots are equiped with a complex sensory-motor system, able to detect the objects and build an analog world model of their location and trajectories (as shown in the right top corner).

and occasionally invent totally new ones. So we need to understand how new aspects of language (new concepts and conceptualisations, new lexical items, new syntactic and semantic categories, new grammatical constructions, new interaction patterns) may arise and spread in a population, the same way biologists try to understand how new life forms may arise (Steels, 2003).

This motivation leads immediately to some requirements. First of all we always use multi-agent simulations so that we can investigate the spreading of conventions in a population. Agents take turns being speaker and hearer and build up competences in conceptualisation and verbalisation (for production) and parsing and interpretation (for understanding). They must be able to store an inventory of rules and apply them in either processing direction, and they must be able to expand their inventories both by inventing new constructions if necessary and by adopting those used by others. Second, the agents must have something to talk about. We are interested in grounded language, which means dialogue about objects and events in the world as perceived through a sensory-motor apparatus. We take embodiment literally. Our experiments use physical robots (Sony AIBOs) located in a real world environment (see figure 1 from (SteelsLoetzsch, 2006)) Third, the agents must be motivated to say and learn something. We achieve this by programming the robots with scripts to play language games. A language game sets up a joint attentional frame so that robots share general motives for interaction, a specific communicative goal (for example draw attention to an object), and give feedback to enable repair of miscommunication (for example through pointing). We typically perform experiments in which a population of agents starts with empty conceptual and linguistic repertoires and then builds from scratch a communication system that is adequate for a particular kind of language game. Agents seek to maximise communicative success while minimising cognitive effort.

One advantage of grounded language experiments is that we can clearly monitor whether the capacities given to the agents are adequate for bootstrapping a language system and how efficient and successful they are. By starting from scratch, we can also test whether our objective of understanding language creativity has been achieved. Of course such experiments will never spontaneously lead to the emergence of English or any other human language, but we can learn a great deal about the processes that have given rise and are still shaping such languages.

3 Meaning

The information about an utterance is organized in a semantic and a syntactic structure. The semantic structure is a decomposition of the utterance's meaning and contains language-specific semantic re-categorisations (for example a put-event is categorised as a cause-move-location with an agent, a patient and a location). The syntactic structure is a decomposition of the form of the utterance into constituents and morphemes and contains additional syntactic categorisations such as syntactic features (like number and gender), word order constraints, etc.

We follow a procedural semantics approach, in the sense that the meaning of an utterance is a program that the hearer is assumed to execute (Winograd, 1972; Johnson-Laird, 1997). Hence conceptualisation becomes a planning process (to plan the program) and interpretation becomes the execution of a program. For example, the meaning of a phrase like "the box" is taken to be a program that involves the application of an image schema to the flow of perceptual images and anchor it to a particular physical object in the scene. So we do not assume some pre-defined or pre-processed logic-style fact base containing the present status of the world (as this is extremely difficult to extract and maintain from real world perception in a noisy and fast changing world) but view language as playing an active role in how the world is perceived and categorised. It is in principle possible to use many different programming languages, but we have opted for constraint based processing and designed a new constraint programming language IRL (Incremental Recruitment Language) and implemented the necessary planning, chunking and execution mechanisms of constraint networks (SteelsBleys, 2005). A simple example of a constraint network for "the box" is as follows[1]:

```
1. (equal-to-context ?s)
2. (filter-set-prototype ?r ?s ?p)
3. (prototype ?p [box])
4. (select-element ?o ?r ?d)
5. (determiner ?d [single-unique])
```

`Equal-to-context`, `select-element`, etc. are primitive constraints that implement fundamental cognitive operators. `Equal-to-context` grabs the set of elements in the current context and binds it to `?s`. `Filter-set-prototype` filters this set with a prototype `?p` which is bound in (3) to `[box]`. `Select-element` selects an element `?o` from `?r` according to the determiner `?d` which is bound to `[single-unique]` in (5), meaning that `?r` should be a singleton. The constraints are powerful enough to be used both in interpretation, when semantic objects such as prototypes, determiners, categories, relations, etc. are supplied through language and values need to be found for other variables, and in conceptualisation, when these values are known but the objective is to find the semantic objects. Moreover, during conceptualization the constraints may extend the repertoire of semantic objects (e.g. introducing a new prototype) if needed, allowing the agents to progressively build up their ontologies.

[1]We use prefix notation. Order does not play a role as the constraint interpreter cycles through the network until all variables are bound or until no further progress can be made. Symbols starting with a question mark represent variables.

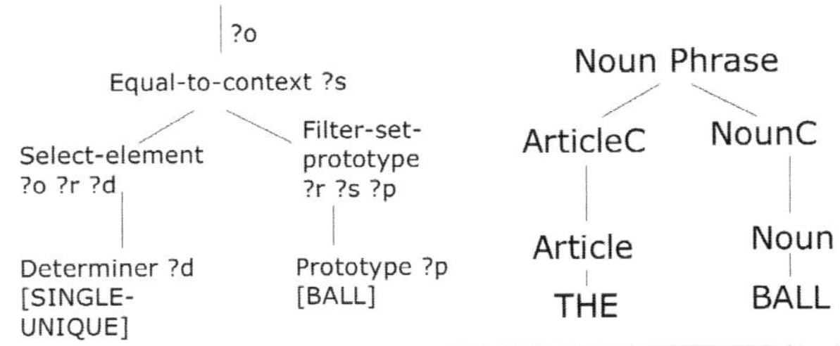

Figure 2: Left: decomposition of the constraint program for "the ball" in the semantic structure. Right: related syntactic structure. In reality both structures contain a lot more information.

4 Syntactic and Semantic Structures

As mentioned, FCG organises the information about an utterance in feature structures, similar to other feature-structure based formalisms (as first introduced by Kay (Kay, 1984)) but with some important differences. An FCG feature structure contains units which correspond (roughly) to words (more precisely morphemes) and constituents.

A unit has a name and a set of features. Hierarchical structure is not implicitly represented by embedding one unit in another one, but explicitly by the features *syn-subunits* (for the syntactic structure) and *sem-subunits* (for the semantic structure). There is a strong correspondence between the syntactic and semantic structure built up for the same utterance (see figure 2) although there can be units which only appear in the syntactic structure (for example for grammatical function words) and vice versa. The correspondence is maintained by using the same unit names in both the semantic and syntactic structure. Units in syntactic structures have three features: (1) *syn-subunits*, (2) *syn-cat* which contains the syntactic categories, and (3) *form* containing the form associated with the unit. Units in semantic structures have four features: (1) *sem-subunits*, (2) *sem-cat* containing the semantic categories, (3) *meaning* which is the part of the utterance's meaning covered by the unit, and (4) *context* which contains variables that occur in the meaning but are 'external' in the sense that they are linked to variables occurring in the meaning of other units. An example semantic structure (in list-notation) for the left structure in figure 2 is shown in figure 3. FCG is a completely open-ended formalism in the sense that all linguistic

```
((unit-1
    (SEM-SUBUNITS (unit-3)))
 (unit-3
    (CONTEXT ((LINK ?s)))
    (MEANING ((EXTERNAL-CONTEXT ?s)))
    (SEM-SUBUNITS (unit-4 unit-5)))
 (unit-4
    (CONTEXT ((LINK ?o ?r)))
    (MEANING ((SELECT-ELEMENT ?o ?r ?d)))
    (SEM-SUBUNITS (unit-6)))
 (unit-5
    (CONTEXT ((LINK ?r ?s)))
    (MEANING ((FILTER-SET-PROTOTYPE ?r ?s ?p)))
    (SEM-SUBUNITS (unit-7)))
 (unit-6
    (CONTEXT ((LINK ?d)))
    (MEANING ((DETERMINER ?d [SINGLE-UNIQUE]))))
 (unit-7
    (CONTEXT ((LINK ?p)))
    (MEANING ((PROTOTYPE ?p [BALL])))))
```

Figure 3: Semantic structure in list-notation.

categories (syntactic or semantic) are open and in principle language-specific (as in radical construction grammar (Croft, 2001).) Thus the set of lexical categories (noun, verb, adjective, etc.), of possible semantic roles (agent, patient, etc.), of syntactic features (number, gender, politeness, etc.), and so on, are all open. The value of the *syn-cat* and *sem-cat* features consists of a conjunction of predicates (each possibly having arguments.) New categories can be introduced at any time and used as (part of) a predicate. The form of the utterance is described in a declarative manner, using predicates like *precedes* or *meets* which define linear ordering relations among the form of units or any other aspect of surface form including prosodic contour or stress.

5 Rules

A rule (also called template) typically expresses constraints on possible meaning-form mappings. Each rule has a score which reflects the success that the agent has had in using it. All else being equal, agents prefer rules with higher scores, thus reflecting frequency effects. A rule has two poles. A left pole which typically contains constraints on semantic structure formulated as a feature structure with variables, and a right pole which typically contains constraints on syntactic structure again formulated as a feature structure with variables. Rules are divided into rule subsets which help constrain the order of rule-application and design large-scale grammars. Thus we make a distinction between morph-rules, which decompose a word into a stem and pending morphemes and introduce syntactic categories; lex-stem-rules, which associate meaning with the stem as well as valence information and a role-frame; con-rules, which correspond to grammatical constructions that associate parts of semantic structure with parts of syntactic structure; and sem and syn-rules which perform inference over semantic or syntactic categories to expand semantic or syntactic structure.

All rules are bi-directional. Typically, during production, the left pole is 'unified' with the semantic structure under construction, possibly yielding a set of bindings. If successful, the right pole is 'merged' with the syntactic structure under construction. The merge operation can be understood as a partial unification, but extending the structure with those parts of the pole that were missing. During parsing, the right pole is unified with the syntactic structure and parts of the left pole are added to the semantic structure. The unification phase is thus used to see whether a rule is triggered and the merge phase represents the actual application of the rule. The FCG Unify and Merge operators are defined in great formal detail in (SteelsDeBeule, 2006). During production lex-stem-rules are applied before the con-rules and the morph-rules. During parsing the lex-stem-rules are applied right after the morph-rules. The con-rules then build higher order structure. It is enormously challenging to write rules that work in both directions but this strong constraint is very helpful to achieve a compact powerful grammar.

6 Building Hierarchy

One of the innovative aspects of FCG is the way it handles hierarchy. Both the left-pole and the right-pole of a construction can introduce hierarchical structure with the J-operator (DeBeuleSteels, 2005). This way, the semantic pole of constructions (lexical or grammatical) can decompose the meaning to be expressed (which originally resides in the top node of the semantic structure) and the syntactic pole can group units together into a larger constituent. Constraints governed by the J-operator do not have to match during the unification phase. Instead they are used to build additional structure during the merge

```
(def-lex-stem-rule put-SVOL
 ((?top
   (meaning
    (==
     (event-type ?event-type
      (put (put-1 ?obj);who
           (put-2 ?obj2);puts what
           (put-3 ?obj3))))));where
  ((J ?new-unit ?top)
   (context
    (== (link ?event-type)))
   (sem-cat
    (==
     (sem-event-type ?event-type
      (cause-move-location
       (agent ?obj)
       (patient ?obj2)
       (location ?obj3)))))))
<-->
 ((?top
   (syn-subunits (== ?new-unit)))
  (?new-unit
   (form
    (== (stem ?new-unit "put"))))
  ((J ?new-unit nil)
   (syn-cat
    (== (valence SVOL))))))
```

Figure 4: Example lexical entry for "put" and illustration of the J-operator.

phase. This may include the construction of a new unit as well as pending from an existing unit and absorbing some other units.

Figure 4 shows an example which will be used further in the next section. It is a lexical rule preparing a resultative construction (GoldbergJackendoff, 2004). The semantic pole of the rule combines some stretch of meaning (the introduction of an event-type, namely a put-event) with a frame (cause-move-location with roles for agent, patient and location). These are associated with a lexical stem "put" in the right pole which also adds a valence frame SVOL (triggering the subject-verb-object-location construction). In production, this rule triggers when a 'put' event-type is part of the meaning ('==' means 'includes but may also contain additional expressions'). When merging the semantic pole with the semantic structure, a new unit hanging from ?top is created and the specified value of the meaning feature copied down. The new unit also receives the context and sem-cat features as specified by the J-operator. At the same time, the syntactic pole is merged with the syntactic structure and so the ?new-unit (which is already bound) is added as a subunit of ?top in the syntactic structure as well. The J-operator will then add stem and valence information. Thus the semantic structure of figure 5 will be transformed into the one of figure 6. And the corresponding syntactic structure becomes as in figure 7. In parsing, an existing syntactic unit with stem

```
((unit-2
  (meaning
   ( ..
     (event-type ev-type1
      (put (put-1 o1) (put-2 o11)
           (put-3 o22))) ... ))))
```

Figure 5: Semantic structure triggering the rule in figure 4 in production.

```
((unit-2
  (sem-subunits (... unit-3 ...)))
 (unit-3
  (meaning
   ((event-type
     ev-type1
     (put (put-1 o1) (put-2 o11)
          (put-3 o22)))))
  (context ((link ev-type1)))
  (sem-cat
   ((sem-event-type
     ev-type1
     (cause-move-location
      (agent o1) (patient o11)
      (location o22))))))
  ... )
```

Figure 6: Resulting semantic structure after applying the rule in figure 4 to the semantic structure of figure 5.

```
((unit-2
  (syn-subunits (... unit-3 ...)))
 (unit-3
  (form ((stem unit-3 "put")))
  (syn-cat ((valence SVOL))))
 ... )
```

Figure 7: Resulting syntactic structure after applying the rule in figure 4.

"put" is required to trigger the rule. If found, the rule will add the valence information to it and on the semantic side the meaning as well as the semantic categorisation in terms of a cause-move-location frame are added.

7 Implementing Constructions

Lexical constructions provide frame and valence information for word stems and parts of meaning. Grammatical constructions bind all this together. Figure 8 shows an example of a grammatical construction. It also uses the J-operator to build hierarchy, both on the semantic side (to decompose or add meaning) and on the syntactic side (to group constituents together.) An example of a SVOL-construct is *Mary puts the milk in the refrigerator*. Before application of the construction, various units should already group together the words making up a nounphrase for the subject (which will be bound to ?subject-unit), a nounphrase for the direct object (bound to the ?object-unit) and a prepositional nounphrase (bound to ?oblique-unit). Each of these units also will bind variables to their referents, communicated as context to the others. On the semantic side the cause-move-location frame with its various roles aids to make sure that all the right variable bindings are established. On the syntactic side the construction imposes word-order constraints (expressed with the meets-predicate), the valence of the verb, and specific types of constituents (nounphrase, verbphrase, prepositional nounphrase). The SVOL construction operates again in two directions. In production it is triggered when the semantic structure built so far unifies with the semantic pole, and then the syntactic structure is expanded with the missing parts from the syntactic pole. Constraints on the syntactic pole (e.g. valence) may prevent the application of the construction. In parsing, the SVOL construction is triggered when the syntactic structure built so far unifies with the syntactic pole and the semantic structure is then expanded with the missing parts from the semantic pole. Again application may be constrained when semantic constraints in the construction prevent it.

8 Fluidity, Conventionalisation and Meta-grammars

Although FCG must become adequate for dealing with the typical phenomena that we find in human natural languages, our main target is to make scientific models of the processes that underly the origins of language, in other words of the creative process by which language users adapt or invent new forms to express new meanings that unavoidably arise in an open world and negotiate tacitly the conventions that they adopt as a group. We have already carried out a number of experiments in this direction and here only a brief summary can be given (for more discussion see: (Steels, 2004; DeBeuleBergen, 2006; SteelsLoetzsch, 2006)).

In our experiments, speaker and hearer are chosen randomly from a population to play a language game as part of a situated embodied interaction that involves perception, joint attention and feedback. When the speaker conceptualizes the scene, he may construct new semantic objects (for example new categories) or recruit new constraint networks in order to achieve the communicative goal imposed by the game. Also when the speaker is trying to verbalise the constraint network that constitutes the meaning of an utterance, there may be lexical items missing or new constructions may have to be built. We use a meta-level architecture with reflection to organise this process. The speaker goes through the normal processing steps, using whatever inventory is available. Missing items may accumulate and then the speaker moves to a meta-level, trying to repair the utterance by stretching existing constructions, re-using them by analogy for new purposes, or introducing other linguistic items. The speaker also engages in self-monitoring by re-entering the utterance and comparing what he meant to say to interpretations derived by parsing his own utterance. The speaker can thus detect potential problems for the listener such as combinatorial explosions in parsing, equalities among variables which were not expressed, etc. and these problems can be repaired by the introduction of additional rules.

The hearer receives an utterance and tries to go as far as possible in the understanding process. The parser and interpreter are not geared towards checking for grammaticality but capable to handle utterances even if a large part of the rules are missing. The (partial) meaning is then used to arrive at an interpretation, aided by the fact that the context and communicative goals are restricted by the language game. If possible, the hearer gives feedback on how he understood the utterance and whether an interpretation was found. If there is failure or miscommunication the hearer will then repair his inventory based on extra information provided by the speaker. This can imply the introduction of new concepts extending the ontology, storing new lexical items, introducing new constructions, assigning certain words to new syntactic classes, etc. Speaker and hearer also update the scores of all rules and concepts. In case of success, scores go up of the items that were used and competitors are decreased to achieve lateral inhibition and hence a positive feedback loop between success and use. In case of failure, scores go down so that the likelihood of using the failing solution diminishes. In our simulations, games are played consecutively by members of a population and we have been able to show –so far for relatively simple forms of language– that shared communication systems can emerge from scratch in populations. Much work remains to be done in researching the repair strategies needed and when they should be triggered. The repair strategies themselves should also be the subject of negotiation among the agents because they make use of a meta-grammar that describes in terms of rules (with the same syntax and processing as the FCG rules discussed here) how repairs are to be achieved.

9 Conclusions

FCG is a tool offered to the community of researchers interested in construction grammar. It allows the precise formal definition of constructions in a unification-based feature structure grammar style and contains the necessary complex machinery for building an utterance starting from meaning and reconstructing meaning starting from an utterance. FCG does not make linguistic theorising superfluous, on the contrary, the formalism is open to any framework of linguistic categories or organisation of grammatical knowledge as long as a construction grammar framework is adopted. There is obviously a lot more to say, not only about how we handle various linguistic phenomena (such as inheritance of properties by a parent phrasal unit from its head subunit) but also what learning operators can progressively build fluid construction grammars driven by the needs of communication. We refer the reader to the growing number of papers that provide more details on these various aspects.

10 Acknowledgement

This research was conducted at the Sony Computer Science Laboratory in Paris and the University of Brussels VUB Artificial Intelligence Laboratory. It is partially sponsored by the EU ECAgents project (FET IST-1940). FCG and the experiments in language evolution are team work and major contributions were made by Joris Bleys, Martin Loetzsch, Nicolas Neubauer, Wouter Van den Broeck, Remy Van Trijp, and Pieter Wellens.

References

Bergen, B.K. and N.C. Chang. (2003) *Embodied Construction Grammar in Simulation-Based Language Understanding.* Technical Report 02-004, International Computer Science Institute, Berkeley.

Clark, H. and S. Brennan (1991) *Grounding in communication.* In: Resnick, L. J. Levine and S. Teasley (eds.) Perspectives on Socially Shared Cognition. APA Books, Washington. p. 127-149.

Croft, William A. (2001). *Radical Construction Grammar; Syntactic Theory in Typological Perspective.* Oxford: Oxford University Press.

De Beule, J. and L. Steels (2005) *Hierarchy in Fluid Construction Grammar.* In: Furbach, U. (eds) (2005) Proceedings of KI-2005. Lecture Notes in AI 3698. Springer-Verlag, Berlin. p.1-15.

De Beule, J. and B. Bergen (2006) *On the Emergence of Compositionality.* Proceedings of the Evolution of Language Conference VI, Rome.

Goldberg, A.E. (1995) *Constructions.: A Construction Grammar Approach to Argument Structure.* University of Chicago Press, Chicago

Goldberg, A. and R. Jackendoff (2004) *The English Resultative as a Family of Constructions.* Language 80 532-568.

Johnson-Laird, P.N. (1997) *Procedural Semantics.* Cognition, 5 (1977) 189-214.

Goldberg, A. (2003) *Constructions: A new theoretical approach to language* Trends in Cognitive Science. Volume 7, Issue 5, May 2003 , pp. 219-224.

Kay, P. and C. Fillmore (1999) *Grammatical constructions and linguistic generalizations: the Whats X doing Y? construction.* Language 75(1), 133.

Kay, M. (1984) *Functional unification grammar: A formalism for machine translation.* Proceedings of the International Conference of Computational Linguistics.

Pollard, C.and I. Sag (1994) *Head-driven Phrase Structure Grammar.* CSLI Stanford Univ, Calif.

Ostman, Jan-Ola and Mirjam Fried (eds.) (2005) *Construction Grammars: Cognitive grounding and theoretical extensions.* W. Benjamins, Amsterdam.

Steels, L. (2003) *Evolving grounded communication for robots.* Trends in Cognitive Science. Volume 7, Issue 7, July 2003 , pp. 308-312.

Steels, L. (2004) *Constructivist Development of Grounded Construction Grammars.* In D. Scott, W. Daelemans and M. Walker (Eds.), Proceedings Annual Meeting of Association for Computational Linguistics Conference. Barcelona: ACL , (pp. 9-16).

Steels, L. and J. De Beule (2006) *Unify and Merge in FCG.* In: Vogt, P. et.al. (eds.) Proceedings of EELC III. Lecture Notes in Computer Science. Springer-Verlag, Berlin.

Steels, L. and J. Bleys (2005) *Planning What To Say: Second Order Semantics for Fluid Construction Grammars.* In: Proceedings of CAEPIA 2005. Santiago de Compostella.

Steels, L. and M. Loetzsch (2006) *Perspective Alignment in Spatial Language.* In: Coventry, K., J. Bateman and T. Tenbrink (2006) Spatial Language in Dialogue. Oxford University Press. Oxford.

Tomasello, M. and P.J. Brooks (1999) *Early syntactic development: A Construction Grammar approach* In: Barrett, M. (ed.) (1999) *The Development of Language* Psychology Press, London. pp. 161-190.

Winograd, T. (1972) *Understanding natural language.* New York, Academic Press.

```
(def-con-rule SVOL-Phrase
  ((?top
     (sem-subunits
       (== ?subject-unit ?verb-unit
        ?object-unit ?oblique-unit)))
   (?subject-unit
     (context (== (link ?subject))))
   (?verb-unit
     (context (== (link ?event ?event-type)))
     (sem-cat
       (== (sem-event-type ?event-type
             (cause-move-location
              (agent ?subject)
              (patient ?object)
              (location ?oblique))))))
   (?object-unit
     (context (== (link ?object))))
   (?oblique-unit
     (context (== (link ?oblique))))
   ((J ?new-unit ?top
       (?subject-unit ?verb-unit
        ?object-unit ?oblique-unit))
     (context (== (link ?event)))))
 <-->
  ((?top
     (form
       (==
        (meets ?subject-unit ?verb-unit)
        (meets ?verb-unit ?object-unit)
        (meets ?object-unit
               ?oblique-unit)))
     (syn-subunits
       (== ?subject-unit ?verb-unit
        ?object-unit ?oblique-unit)))
   (?subject-unit
     (syn-cat
       (== (constituent NounPhrase))))
   (?verb-unit
     (syn-cat
       (== (constituent VerbPhrase)
           (valence SVOL))))
   (?object-unit
     (syn-cat
       (== (constituent NounPhrase))))
   (?oblique-unit
     (syn-cat
       (== (constituent PrepNounPhrase))))
   ((J ?new-unit ?top
       (?subject-unit ?verb-unit
        ?object-unit ?oblique-unit))
     (syn-cat
       (== (constituent sentence))))))
```

Figure 8: A resultative construction.

Author Index

Association for Computational Linguistics
209 N. Eighth Street
Stroudsburg, Pennsylvania 18360